ELEVATING YOURSELF FOR SUCCESS

A LEADERSHIP PERSPECTIVE

NANCY MERCURIO

Strategic Book Publishing
New York, New York

Strategic Book Publishing
An imprint of AEG Publishing Group
845 Third Avenue, 6th Floor – 6016
New York, NY 10022
http://www.strategicbookpublishing.com

ISBN: 978-1-60860-634-4

Printed in the United States of America

Book Design: Suzanne Kelly

Dedications

This book is dedicated to the leaders around the globe who shared their challenges and successes during coaching, consulting, and training sessions over the past decade. These collective experiences, and the common threads between them, provided the knowledge and proven methods shared throughout this book. It has been an honor to serve every person, and organization who ever entrusted me with guiding individual and organizational success.

To future leaders: May you have the patience and fortitude to learn from your mistakes, the ability to make the growth and development of others a top priority, and be willing to change your behaviors to become more effective in serving the organizations that have invested in you. May you also be willing to learn from those leaders who have laid the foundation for your success.

To my husband who has been a confidant, personal editor, objective critic, and best friend; thank you for your endless support of my work and for your tireless efforts to help individuals and organizations become more effective and productive.

To my Mom who left this earth during the final stages of this book: Thank you for your valuable insights and for always providing perspective throughout my life. You were an inspiration and guiding light in all endeavors.

Nancy Mercurio

Table of Contents

Introduction

The role of the leader at every level is critical to the success of any organization. Every environment including for-profit, non-profit, service and product-related organizations, all rely upon their leaders to provide the tactical and strategic guidance necessary to drive business objectives. No role has a greater impact on an organization than the actions of the leader. With one decision, a leader can set success or disaster into motion and affect numerous people in the process.

While there are countless, valuable books on the topic of leadership; few have ever approached the most important aspect of leadership: *the ability to gain perspective in every situation before taking action.*

The title denotes a core theme referenced throughout the book: *acquiring an elevated view.* The analogy used to demonstrate this concept is an elevator; *taking the elevator to a higher floor,* represents removing oneself from the current environment to gain perspective. Most people have been in an elevator at some point in their lives and subsequently, can relate to the concept of what an elevator provides. It is an immediate escape from surrounding activities and offers momentary peace of mind. When the doors open and one exits the elevator, people and situations are different, which provides the opportunity to gain new perspective.

Elevating Yourself For Success, is focused on learning how to become an objective observer at all times, in order to determine the best plan of action for handling any issue. Acquiring perspective before taking action is directly correlated to favorable outcomes in all aspects of leadership such as delegation, communication, coaching, relationships, individual and organizational growth, and development.

The topics for the chapters included in this book emerged as a result of tracking the most common challenges faced by leaders who were either coaching clients or training participants. For nearly two decades, notes taken during client engagements led to a clear understanding that the same problems existed amongst leaders, regardless of the environments in which they served.

This book is written in a straightforward, hard-hitting style that eliminates the guesswork on how to incorporate perspective into daily activities. The book also provides guidance to assist the reader in application of learning by providing a host of recommended actions in each respective subject.

The methods described in the contents of the book are designed to help the inexperienced leader as well as the savviest leader, and are guaranteed to enlighten anyone who embraces its concepts. Most importantly, learning to acquire the behaviors described in this book will indeed lead to successful outcomes in individual and organizational success.

If becoming a more effective leader is your goal, then you will undeniably find the book useful in Elevating Yourself For Success!

CHAPTER 1

An Unproductive Day

TUESDAY 10:00 A.M.

Your team has a critical presentation to deliver on Wednesday at 8:30 a.m. to an audience of 150 key leaders. This presentation will be the first of many, and will introduce the rollout of a new process that impacts the entire organization.

To date, you have held four meetings with all seven of your Direct Reports. In the first meeting, you served as facilitator and discussed the following:
Target audience, project goals, the desired response from your audience, and the visibility this project brings to you and to the team.

The remaining three meetings were held at various intervals during the following ten weeks, as the project progressed. Although you attended those meetings, your role was strictly in an advisory capacity; providing guidance where needed, and answering questions only when answers from the team were not forthcoming.

During all four meetings, you demonstrated your trust and faith in the team's abilities; individually and collectively. Throughout this project, you have delivered a consistent message of encouraging individuals to be as creative as they desired with the presentation itself.

Although at one of the earlier meetings you casually mentioned your interest in wanting to preview the final presentation deck before the big day, you also made a point of stating that this was not a requirement. No additional comments were shared with the team regarding your interest or need to see or approve the presentation prior to its unveiling.

~~~~~~

The clock is ticking, and the first delivery to key constituents is less than 24 hours from now. You have yet to hear if the presentation has been finalized, and to date, have not seen a draft or copy. As your concerns escalate, you begin to question whether the group is truly prepared.

What action should you take?

Do you make an inquiry phone call, send a simple email, casually ask the question while getting your coffee, or continue to draw a variety of conclusions based on lack of information?

Determining the most effective action to take is critical to your credibility as a leader, and it is in these situations that the biggest mistakes are typically made. Acting out of fear, or without consideration for the impact your actions will have on the team is risky, and could cause irreversible damage to teaming efforts.

As a leader in these situations, your credibility and reputation depend upon your ability to *gain perspective before taking action*. Timing is everything given the upcoming presentation and the team's momentum in crossing the finish line.

To help demonstrate this point, consider the following options for taking action and the potential outcomes associated with each.

Option 1

Action: *Make an inquiry call.*
Phone the person you consider to be least likely to overreact, and leave a voicemail asking how things are going, never mentioning the actual presentation. At the same time, ask if there is anything you can do to help.

Potential Outcome:
The individual returns your call and leaves a voicemail saying *thanks, but we are all set.*

Effectiveness:
This option will likely not satisfy your curiosity, nor provide you with the security of knowing how well prepared the group is for tomorrow's meeting.

Option 2

Action: *Send an email.*
Send an email to one of the project leaders stating that while everything is likely under control, you are simply reaching out to see if the group needs anything.

Potential Outcomes:
You receive an *Out of Office* reply for this individual. Subsequently, you panic at the thought that this individual is not even at work today!

~~~~~~

Rather than pick one option over the other, you initiate both in this case, and the actions set in motion are as follows:

> You left a voicemail for one individual who in turn responds via voicemail stating that everything is completed.

You emailed a second individual and received an *Out of Office* reply.

Two actions taken and two individuals impacted at this point.

In the meantime, it turns out that the individual you emailed actually did receive the message and in turn, forwarded it on to the remainder of the team soliciting their needs. Unaware that the *Out of Office* reply message remains activated from the previous week's travels, the individual waits for responses from others before replying to you.

TUESDAY 12:30 P.M.

You are scheduled to be in a meeting with your boss and peers on unrelated business from 3:00 p.m. to 5:00 p.m. Your concerns are escalating, and in fact, this issue is consuming your thoughts. While you are desperately trying not to overreact, you decide to reach out via email to another person on the team.

The third action you take is to send a second email.

Three individuals have been contacted directly, and all seven are involved at this point.

Your second email is sent to someone who had already received the forwarded first email, unbeknownst to you. This individual then forwards the second email received to the entire team with the following additional commentary:
What's the deal with Harry? He must really be nervous to have sent out two emails today checking on us!

In the meantime, the individual who received your voicemail responds to the peer forwarded email stating the following:

I received a phone call from Harry earlier today asking the same, and I left him a voicemail stating that we were all set. Is he still asking?

During conversations to finalize the plan for the presentation tomorrow, individuals on the team exchange theories on what is driving your overt efforts. All agree that no assistance is needed with the presentation at this time, and that they prefer surprising you with their creativity at tomorrow's meeting.

~~~~~~

TUESDAY 3:00 P.M.

While you proceed to your meeting, your thoughts are preoccupied with the team and concerns for whether or tomorrow's presentation will be a success or a disaster. Frustrations increase, and you are mentally revisiting all actions to date during this entire project to uncover gaps in the process.

TUESDAY 5:15 P.M.

You check email and read a response sent from the recipient of your first email earlier this day, (the individual who had the *Out of Office* reply message activated).

The response reads as follows:

Thanks Harry. We finalized the details today for tomorrow's presentation and everyone agrees that we are all set; no assistance needed, but thanks for asking.

Nancy Mercurio

This email response is similar to the voicemail you received earlier, and again, does not satisfy or ease your concerns. Given there is no presentation attached to the email, you hit *Reply to All*. The message you craft clearly states how disappointed you are that you have yet to view the planned presentation for tomorrow's meeting. Additionally, you share that given the visibility of this project, you expected far more from this team.

Your email sparks greater concern amongst the team, and now with less than 13 hours until the kickoff, everyone is discussing your email and your behaviors rather than the delivery of the presentation.

To illustrate the results of your efforts, let's revisit the highlights of the outcomes from your actions this day:

The entire day was spent distracted, disorganized, stressed, and ultimately less productive than you can afford to be, given your workload. There was little you could contribute to the meeting you attended with your boss, and peers given the preoccupation you were experiencing related to your team.

Equally important to note is that the team was unnecessarily sidetracked from preparing themselves for the big day. Rather than focusing their energy on audience needs and fine-tuning their presentation, your messages took precedence this day. Their conversations with one another instead surrounded uncovering what triggered your concerns.

Additionally, they have begun questioning whether your support of them throughout this project has been genuine from the onset. Subsequently, the events of this day will most definitely impact future projects, as they will be apprehensive to trust your intentions as initially stated.

8

What went wrong?

The bottom line in this case is that you failed to clarify specific expectations in a forthright manner. While you were certainly entitled to review the presentation prior to delivery, at no time did you directly ask for the opportunity to do so. Nor did you provide a date for the submission of this information.

Lack of clarification and communication related to desired results, caused an undesirable and ineffective set of events that will have long-term impact on future teaming efforts.

CONSIDER YOUR NEEDS

Making your expectations for participation clear at the onset of any project is imperative, but they must also be realistic. Level of participation should be based on knowledge of your own operating style and behavioral tendencies.

Through asking yourself some simple questions, it is easy to determine what would have worked better for you in this situation:

Question #1: *What level of participation would have made you most comfortable?*

In this scenario, it would have been wiser to communicate one of your expectations as needing to review, edit, and approve the presentation prior to final delivery. No doubt given your concerns, having access to the final presentation would have minimized frustration.

Nancy Mercurio

Question #2: *Where does your trust begin and end?*

It would have been best to explain that regardless of their talents and experience, any project with high visibility places you and the team at risk. Closer involvement simply helps you feel more secure, and prepared, and in no way translates to having a lack of trust in their abilities.

~~~~~~

In an attempt to build loyalty and instill confidence in the team, you compromised your need to be totally confident and comfortable. As the deadline approached, you behaved in ways that minimized your credibility. Your behaviors also negated previous efforts to build loyalty and confidence amongst the team.

Acting hastily is driven by the desire to yield results in a timely manner.

Yet, it is acting with haste that is often counterproductive to maximizing contributions from those we hire.

Understanding how your actions impact individuals and the organization is where our journey together begins....

CHAPTER 2

Gaining Perspective:
An Elevator View

Regardless of the type of challenges you face each day, your ability to gain perspective before taking action is key to determining what behaviors are most likely to drive successful outcomes.

In every challenge, personal or professional, thinking and acting with objectivity should be a priority. Speaking or saying anything before you can assess the consequences of potential actions can be detrimental to your reputation, and can devalue your relationships.

Learning to become an objective observer provides an opportunity to view all aspects of one situation such as your role, expectations, (stated and implied), risk factors, timelines, and the capabilities of those involved. Such clarity is necessary in determining which behaviors or actions will elicit desired outcomes.

We have all experienced the wrath of someone who is too quick to respond or too shortsighted in a situation. These individuals tend to draw immediate conclusions before uncovering the facts, overreacting without fully understanding the situation.

Nancy Mercurio

Equally painful are the memories we have of our own inappropriate actions when acting hastily without information. Those on the receiving end of our behaviors are likely to recall these experiences in the same painful manner.

Acquiring an objective perspective sounds simple, but for individuals who are more accustomed to having knee-jerk reactions and for those driven by emotions, it is anything but simple.

No doubt, you can recall a situation or confrontation in which gaining perspective would have prevented undesirable consequences. These situations literally take more time to resolve than the time they take to initiate.

In every situation, personal or professional, the ability to acquire immediate objectivity is critical to understanding one another. It is the difference between volatile and peaceful outcomes. Gaining objectivity prevents us from overreacting or becoming the victim of someone who is.

Also important to note is that in every decision, the presence of perspective and objectivity ensures that all possible and subsequent outcomes are considerations in determining the best approach.

The greatest frustrations of any leader can frequently be attributed to the inability to perceive the big picture, or working with someone who lacks this capability.

Imagine the perspective you would gain if you could rise above the situation, almost as though you were having an out of body experience! It would be an opportunity to serve as an objective observer in your own scenario; a chance to see all sides immediately before responding.

For visual learners, it is easier to grasp this concept by creating a mental image. Phrases such as *Beam Me Up Scotty* or *Calgon Take Me Away* provide easily accessible mental images that help us remove ourselves from the immediate chaos at hand.

This book proposes yet another phrase or image for gaining immediate objectivity:

Take the Elevator Up!

Picture yourself waiting for an elevator. The noise levels surrounding you are high as you can literally hear bits and pieces of numerous conversations. The steady stream of shoes walking across the tiled floor is creating a drumbeat in your head.

Then suddenly, the doors of the elevator open and you and three others step into the elevator. While you may not be alone, you are quick to recognize these golden moments of silence and the chance to breathe in the calm. It is indeed a moment of Zen.

In only a matter of minutes, you step away from the hustle and bustle and are into the silence. The elevator concept demonstrates the value of taking a few moments to collect your thoughts and consider the potential impact of your words or actions. It is a visual image that can easily be referenced.

Consider how much easier each day would be if you could manage those minutes or seconds of chaos, avoiding premature responses! Imagine the difference it would make if you could learn to appreciate the value of stepping away long enough to gain perspective.

Nancy Mercurio

In order to know if this method can help you, consider how you might answer the following questions:

- How many situations rob you of your peace or knock you off your foundation each day?

- How easily are you rattled?

- How quick are you to overreact or respond based upon what you think happened or should have happened, without knowing all the facts?

Establishing the practice of mentally *Taking the Elevator Up,* is paramount to preventing actions before gaining clarity of the situation at hand.

Picture any Embassy Suites Hotel, where each floor has a circular style design; all rooms facing an open area in the center where activities below are easily viewed while overlooking a balcony.

The ground floor has a lobby area where the entrance, restaurants, hotel sales offices, sitting areas, waterfalls or other such foliage are located. This floor is typically the busiest area in the hotel. People are entering and exiting the doors, crossing the lobby or standing in line to check in or check out; servers are busy serving the guests in the open area restaurants, and guests are actively holding conversations. While words cannot be deciphered, the humming sound from multiple conversations is consistent.

Now imagine you and a colleague are checking into the hotel for a convention you are attending. There are over 100 people standing in the lobby, some visiting with one another while others are checking in as well.

You and your colleague decide to stand in separate check-in lines and before you know it, the two of you cannot see one another through the crowd. Locating your colleague is a challenge given the fact that you are both on the ground floor.

To quickly gain perspective, you *take the elevator up* to the next floor. As you stand looking over the balcony, you can easily see people milling around. Within seconds, you locate your colleague.

Running around the lobby looking for this person would have made it more difficult to gain perspective. *Taking the Elevator Up* offered an improved perspective and objectivity.

~~~~~~

Another example to demonstrate this point is overhearing a conversation in which you are unable to actually see the two individuals involved. While you are unaware of the facial expressions or other such body language being displayed, you can clearly hear the emotion being expressed through the vocal intonations and intensity of the words as they are spoken.

Immediately following this verbal exchange, one of the individuals approaches you regarding the conversation that just occurred, unaware of the fact that you overheard the conversation. This person proceeds to share their perspective of the negative verbal exchange with no admission of responsibility for having played a role in the situation.

Having been privy to the conversation, you are rather quick to admit that indeed you actually heard much of the conversation. You further explain that based upon what you overheard, both parties were responsible for the outcome.

It is important to note that had you been an eyewitness to the conversation, you might not have gained the objectivity you were able to share with this individual. In fact, it is more likely that a visual sideline position would have blinded you from seeing both individuals as contributors.

Creating the distance you need to be an observer in any situation prevents you from acting in ways that are emotionally induced.

Consider the impact of operating without an elevator perspective in the following scenario:

SITUATION

Imagine you just received a call from a peer telling you that one of your direct reports was overheard talking about you in the cafeteria.

Responding *Without* Perspective:

A gut reaction in this case is to assume the worse when learning that someone is speaking negatively about you. Dozens of fleeting thoughts run through your mind; the last exchange with this person; kind gestures you have expressed; times you have acted beyond the call of duty to support this individual, etc.

You have quickly formulated an opinion about the behavior, acquired an attitude, and are likely wondering how to handle yourself during the next encounter with this individual.

At this point, your thoughts are not factually based and are instead being driven by your emotions.

Responding *With* Perspective:

You receive the same call from a peer regarding having overheard one of your direct reports talking about you; however, this time, you RUN FOR THE ELEVATOR BEFORE speaking! You are quickly elevated to a higher level, refusing to react or take action before learning the facts.

Once you are in a mental space where you can take an observer's view, you find yourself able to consider an entirely different perspective such as the following:

- What was the purpose of your peer sharing this information?
- What specifically was overheard?
- Who was your direct report speaking to?

Another option, once you have perspective, is to affirm to the peer that your relationship with this direct report has been positive, and that you prefer to trust that anything said was done with good intentions.

You could also inform the direct report to be more cautious at lunch when using your name, and leave it at that. Most importantly, refrain from demonstrating any emotion while sharing the information. If the direct report feels the need, he or she will inform you as to intentions behind the conversation.

The concept of *Taking the Elevator Up* is an opportunity to choose your viewing floor according to your preferred level of involvement. The higher the level, the more removed you are from the details, subsequently providing greater perspective. Determining the preferred level of involvement should be based on desire for employee autonomy, concern for organizational visibility of the activity, timing of business objectives, etc.

17

Nancy Mercurio

It's all about perspective and the importance of *gaining objectivity before taking action.*

~~~~~~

Why is perspective so important?

Think back to any serious or intense conversation you recently had. Recall if you will, the details that led to one of the more defining moments in the scene, and ask yourself the following questions:

- How did the views, the comments, or the actions of the other person negatively impact how you responded, reacted, or resolved this situation?

- How did your views, comments, or actions negatively influence how you responded, reacted, or resolved this situation?

Now, consider asking yourself another question:

- How would this situation have improved if you could have distanced yourself long enough to gain perspective?

Most of us do not react to what others say or do, but rather to our interpretation of what others say or do.

More importantly, none of us enjoy being on the receiving end of the person who is quick to respond with their interpretation of our words.

Perspective is about objectivity; a chance to see the 'big picture' in any situation where you have become so immersed in the details that you cannot see clearly.

~~~~~~

Consider a crowded movie theatre. When the movie is over and everyone starts to leave, the exit paths become very congested. If you attended the movie with your significant other or a family member, the first thing you might do is reach for their hand or find another means of connecting until you can move through the crowd to the first opening. In this situation, it is simply impossible to see what lies ahead while proceeding through the crowded corridor.

The same is true when you are driving down the highway behind a semi-truck. Most drivers try desperately to find the first opening in which to pass the truck for a clearer view of the road.

The point is this; there are moments when the view is blocked for whatever reason, and clarity is only moments away.

Waiting for an improved perspective can prevent ineffective behaviors and undesirable outcomes.

Most importantly, consider the amount of time and energy required to implement the corrective actions necessary to counteract your ineffective behaviors. It is often a never-ending battle.

The real challenge is not only in how to gain instant access to an objective perspective, but also in honing the skills to incorporate this practice into one's standard mode of operations.

Learning to better manage those moments when clarity is needed is the perfect opportunity to eliminate ineffective reactions, and increase favorable responses.

CHAPTER 3

The Inability to Remain Objective

Understanding what prevents objectivity is just as important as learning how to remain objective. Emotions, communication skills, past experiences, relationships, and fear are all contributing factors to our inability to remain objective. Awareness to these obstacles can help you gain perspective before the circumstances in any situation induce an emotional reaction.

How do emotions impact objectivity?

Everyone has emotional triggers; often referred to as the buttons that get pushed just far enough to elicit our worst responses. Emotional triggers include people or subjects to which we are emotionally attached, regardless of the reason behind the attachment.

In leadership, emotional responses are frequently triggered by the disappointment we experience when others fail to meet our expectations. Behaviors associated with any of the following three key factors can trigger such disappointment:

1. Desire for others to succeed;
   Particularly when we have invested time and energy in someone we believe has potential.

2. End result differing from expectation;
   When we depend upon others to deliver certain results, especially in situations where expectations were communicated; (or so we perceive), and results are less than anticipated.

3. Betrayal or disrespect;
   Anytime an individual misrepresents our intentions, outwardly behaves the opposite of communicated intentions, or demonstrates a lack of respect, especially in public.

Each of these three areas has enormous impact on our emotional triggers and can ultimately prevent our ability to remain objective. Regardless of whether perceived or real, the mere implication that we are somehow being let down can trigger the response. We invest in others and in turn anticipate mutual investment in the form of contribution and respect.

Let's face it; we expect others to behave in the same manner we would in similar circumstances. When that doesn't happen, we are quick to judge the behavior, assimilate it as personally intended, and of course point out how we would have managed the situation; with or without valid similar experience. Being personally invested in another individual or in an outcome makes it difficult to see the forest through the trees!

An even greater problem is that our emotional responses and/or reactions are typically experienced or displayed BEFORE all of the facts have been uncovered, as is demonstrated in the following scenario:

> You entrust a direct report (Bob) with crucial information regarding the potential of a new project being assigned to your team. During the conversation, you clearly explain that this is only a potential assignment, and if awarded to your team, you plan to assign it to him.
>
> The next day during a staff meeting, another direct report (Sue) asks you in front of everyone what potential projects are on the horizon.
>
> Your initial thoughts are that Bob must have leaked the information to Sue and you are furious. You then lash out at Sue in front of the group reminding her that given her team is behind on their current project right now, she should just focus on her own work.
>
> The rest of the meeting is a bit stressful for everyone who has no idea what caused you to snap at Sue, and from that point forward, the meeting is a one-way communication.
>
> Following the meeting, you ask Bob to meet you in your office. When he arrives, you ask him if he shared the information with Sue that you had shared with him. He responds by telling you that he didn't tell her anything about the upcoming project.
>
> He further explains that she told him earlier that she thinks the department is at risk because no new projects are being assigned. He tells you that he merely responded to her by stating that you don't share her concerns. He claims that's all he said to her.

Regardless, you feel betrayed and you aren't sure you believe him. You trusted Bob, even after having suspected he was not trustworthy when he first arrived two years ago. While you had no proof to substantiate your suspicions, it took you months to feel you could share information with him and are now skeptical that he can be trusted.

This situation will have a lasting impact on your relationship with Bob unless you can gain perspective. Taking a totally objective view, you would clearly see that you responded to Sue unfairly because you were preoccupied by the conclusions you were drawing. Perhaps she really just asked because she was concerned about not having work on the horizon. Had you focused solely on the facts, you would have maintained your composure and simply answered her question.

As for Bob, you have two choices:

1. You can believe him and trust that no further evidence will surface, or

2. You can choose not to believe him and spend months suspecting him.

What are the risks associated with each choice?

In looking at the facts, disregarding suspicions, there is no risk in believing him. However, there are greater risks in disbelieving him because it can lower productivity, negatively impact what appears to be a good relationship at this point, and you risk the impact this could have on the team he leads.

It's your choice how to view the situation but weighing out the risks definitely shows your best option is to believe him and apologize to Sue for the outburst.

Nancy Mercurio

What role does communication play in preventing objectivity?

The greatest challenge lies in the difference between what you said and what others heard, and vice versa. Unless the conversation was videotaped or recorded, details related to how, what, where and when, are left to personal recall and interpretation; and ultimately perception.

Each of us knows only too well, the frustrations associated with having another person provide their version of a particular message we communicated. It becomes virtually impossible to remain objective when being misquoted or misrepresented or at the very least, perceiving that to be the case.

Yet, when you consider that on average, only 8% of communication is interpreted from actual words used, it is easy to understand why there can be misinterpretations and misunderstandings.

Unless the communication is stated, restated, and then recited by the other party immediately upon hearing it, there is no guarantee that both individuals walk away with the same perspective. Even then, there is the potential for misinterpretation of the intention behind the words; such as communicating a request as being 'critically important' without providing a completion date.

The most effective means of eliminating communication as an obstacle preventing objectivity is to avoid one-way communications; verbal or written. Verbal exchanges should be followed up in writing, and written communications should require responses. Taking these extra steps is still no guarantee for improved understanding; however, such effort will assist in minimizing misinterpretation.

Above all, when problems occur, rise above the problems to gain perspective. Focusing on who said what to who is unlikely to resolve anything. Instead, *maintain focus on how to resolve the difference between what is and what adjustments are needed to drive desired outcomes.* The rest is history...

How do past experiences affect objectivity?

The quickest way to answer this question is to ask yourself how easy it is for you to trust someone after they have fallen short of expectations; personally or professionally.

Negative experiences far outweigh the positive ones when it comes to accessing the mental images we have stored. Consequently, it takes only a second or two to be quickly reminded of the dangers associated with depending upon the same individual who previously left a permanent emotional or mental scar. Worse yet is that the negative experiences recalled have often occurred months or even years ago.

Let's fast-forward two years on the Bob scenario and consider how the past could influence the current response:

> You have the perfect assignment for someone with Bob's skills. In fact, he is the only person on your team with the experience and knowledge to implement this initiative successfully. However, because this project will require the project leader to interact with some key individuals in the organization, you have reservations about choosing Bob for several reasons:
>
> First, Bob has never worked with these individuals before and doing so, he will be privy to highly confidential information. In addition, his behaviors with these individuals will indeed be a reflection on you.

In looking at the facts objectively, you would have to consider the following:

- Bob has not acted in any way contrary to what he said when he told you he did not tell Sue the information two years ago.

- Bob has the knowledge and skill set needed for the role.

- His success in this role would indeed reflect well on you.

If you understand that the brain most readily recalls experiences that have had a painful impact, you can see the value of taking time to determine whether the recalled image is a fair assessment of the current situation.

When human factors are considered, ours as well as theirs, it becomes easier to give someone a second chance to win your trust or redeem themselves. However, giving someone a second chance requires the willingness to be completely open minded about the potential for success. Otherwise, it's nothing more than a second chance doomed to failure.

Keep in mind that it is easy to perceive any sign of similarity (behavior or circumstance), as being indicative of a pending repeat performance before the outcome is clear. The goal is to remain objective until the individual crosses the finish line or the final outcomes can be assessed.

The ultimate challenge lies in your willingness to conduct a fair and objective evaluation of each experience, along with the relevance each has to the previous one.

What role does fear play in preventing objectivity?

Fear can be mentally and emotionally paralyzing, especially when it comes to perception. Anytime we perceive the behaviors of others as somehow threatening our safety, security, or success, it becomes difficult to remain objective.

The problem with fear is that it impacts each person differently. Some people live their life in fear and therefore are suspecting of everyone's intentions. Others are fearful of little and therefore are overly trusting of the intentions of others.

Somewhere in between these two extremes is the best position to take, because you can still be objective enough to consider how the fear factor is overshadowing reality.

What you perceive as threatening behavior has everything to do with how confident you are in your role, the value of the contributions you make, and your ability to assess facts.

For example:

> If one of your direct reports challenges you on decisions and you are able to maintain focus on the concerns the individual is expressing, you can easily address the issues.

> Conversely, if you are focused on feeling threatened by the challenge, you will defend your decisions and ignore the individual's concern. Subsequently, the individual's actions become more blatant and you become more threatened.

27

The fear we experience is connected to the intentions of others and our perception around those intentions. While it is impossible to avoid fear factors, evaluating the source of your fears will help you understand and ultimately work through them. As you evaluate the source, you begin to recognize how perception often outweighs reality.

To overcome fears, you must conduct an objective evaluation of the facts, consider the impact of perception on those facts, and remove any emotional attachment to the facts.

Circumstances surrounding any given situation can prevent us from having a clear perspective. Therefore, you must learn to distance yourself from the situation long enough to gain clarity and act in accordance.

Identifying and acknowledging the impact of key contributing factors is the best way to begin gaining perspective in all situations.

CHAPTER 4

Delegation and Desired Outcomes

Leaders spend the greater part of each work day direct-ing employees to execute business activities. It is one of the most important functions of leadership and has the greatest impact on the business. Yet, even with its critical importance to business success, assignments are often delegated devoid of suitable preparations or clear com-munications. While some leaders believe the success in delegation lies with the individual performing the tasks, there is actually much more to consider in the process.

Many employees work aimlessly all day performing assignments; unable to connect the dots between what they are accomplishing and the impact to business. Work is often assigned without conversation occurring around the purpose of the task, and little time is available for questions to be asked. With work that is assigned via email, there is even less opportunity for conversation.

From an employee perspective, knowing the value of the task can often serve as the catalyst for delivering excellence. When an employee understands how their contributions add value to the business, they perceive themselves as being valuable. Such perception leads to improved performance, long-term commitments and increased loyalty, and is the very essence of driving suc-cessful outcomes.

Nancy Mercurio

Communicating purpose, expectations, and desired results is the only sure way to maximize outcomes and avoid expending countless hours implementing corrective actions. It is also a positive means of avoiding inevitable disappointments in people and outcomes.

Unclear Expectations + Lack of Communication = DISASTER, every time!

Whether assigning responsibility, selecting individuals for teams or addressing a problem, communicating specifically what needs to be accomplished coupled with the intended outcome, must serve as the core of all interactions and decisions.

Let's look at an example that demonstrates this point:

Perhaps you have an employee you are considering promoting but first need greater insight into the individual's capability. There's an upcoming project that would be the perfect assignment to allow you to observe how this individual best operates. More importantly, the skills this individual would need for the assignment are similar to those needed to perform the potential new role.

Performing this assignment would also open the door for the employee to communicate knowledge and reach out for help in areas less familiar. Doing so would provide you with insights related to knowledge, skills, and areas for growth and development.

While it may be premature to mention the potential promotion, it is certainly reasonable to convey your desire for greater visibility to the individual's skill set. Communicating that this assignment would challenge ability and likely be energizing in the process would also be beneficial.

Conveying interest in leveraging talents is motivating to employees, regardless of whether or not a potential promotion is a factor. By sharing the intention behind the assignment, the individual is privy to the desired result, which in turn creates a sense of enthusiasm. The assignment then becomes a chance to showcase talents versus simply taking on yet another task. Without communicating intention, you risk being disappointed in the employee's efforts in spite of a favorable finish; while at the same time, the individual misses the opportunity to demonstrate greater value. No winners emerge in the process.

In every assignment or delegation, the focus should be on leveraging talents to accomplish results. Communicating intention increases the likelihood that talents will emerge in the process. Capitalizing on individual strengths should be deemed as important as achieving desired results. When these two components are considered equally valuable, growth and development can occur.

Outlining and communicating desired outcomes could eliminate most of the troubleshooting efforts that consume the leader's day. Taking the time necessary at the onset of an assignment should be considered preventive maintenance as it would indeed reduce time spent on corrective actions.

Consider the following example that highlights this point:

> You have ten employees who have successfully worked together in mapping a plan for an initiative to drive organizational change. In fact, their plan is ready for review five days ahead of the scheduled due date.

To impress you, the team has set up a meeting with key constituents to discuss the details of their plan and they have copied you on the email distribution list. The meeting is scheduled for tomorrow afternoon.

While you are pleased with their efforts on the project, there is a moment of panic when you see who is on the distribution list. Your expectation was that it would be you, and you alone who had the first opportunity to fully evaluate the completed plan. However, in a quick and objective review of your initial statements, you realize that you failed to communicate your desire to the team. Now, you are in a potentially embarrassing situation and decide to hold an emergency meeting with the team before they share the plan with others outside your group.

Once you have made these initial assessments, you must take action. The next move you make can change the climate of the team and impact momentum. There are two alternative approaches to the message you convey:

Alternative 1: *You email the following message to all ten team members:*

It is imperative that we meet prior to the plan being shared with others. Tomorrow morning, 7:00 a.m is a mandatory meeting for all team members. Conference Room 7B.

Needless to say, this message will have an immediate impact on the spirit of this group that has experienced tremendous success together. Failure to communicate your expectations upfront will minimize the enthusiasm experienced by the team in preparing for the upcoming meeting with constituents.

Alternative 2: *You email a different message to all ten members:*

While you are certainly entitled to be the first to review the plan, this need must be conveyed in a way to avoid impacting momentum. The second email below is an improved expression and will have little to no impact:

> *I'm impressed that you are prepared to share the plan. Great job everyone! I would like the opportunity to see and discuss the presentation before the meeting with our key leaders. I'm available tomorrow from 1 – 3 if some of you could meet to review this with me. All are welcomed but given this is such short notice I'd appreciate at least one or two of you meeting with me. Please let me know who is available.*
>
> *Thanks in advance for your time, and again, congrats on a great job!*

In the revised message, the objective to review the plan in advance of the big meeting is accomplished, and the team remains focused on the upcoming meeting with the constituents.

ASSIGNING DUTIES

Some leaders delegate according to who is available at the time, while others delegate solely based upon talent. There are advantages and disadvantages to both as outlined below:

Delegating Based Upon Availability

　　Advantages
- Immediate action can be taken
- Allows the task to be immediately addressed

Disadvantages
- May or may not leverage talent
- Could require corrective actions
- May require increased oversight

Delegating Based Upon Talent
Advantages
- Most capable person performs the task
- Knowledge exists for troubleshooting
- Less likelihood for failure

Disadvantages
- Individual growth/development may be limited
- Fewer challenging opportunities available for others

Both options can provide value and although timing may be the priority, leaders should capitalize when possible on opportunities for growth and development to occur.

Regardless of which approach you take, there are key elements to consider in making any assignment:
- What decision-making authority will this individual have?
- What parameters exist with this assignment?
- Are others working on this or something similar?
- What resources are available; financial, human, materials?
- Which areas of this assignment do you want or need to participate in?
- When is the desired completion date or time?

While most of these factors are frequently addressed when the questions or challenges arise, it is usually after negative actions have already been set into motion. At that point, far too much energy is expended on damage control.

Both the employee and the leader are impacted by a lack of proper planning, and in fact, the efforts of one person can easily affect an entire department. Such situations create frustration and minimize productivity, causing interruptions to the day.

Lack of planning can also lead to employees feeling micromanaged, as leaders must then step in to make decisions with every obstacle. Once the employee feels micromanaged, there is little to no desire to take initiative or act without first seeking guidance. At this point in the scenario, the employee is a laborer performing a task and returning to the leader for instructions at every turn.

What decision-making authority will this individual have?

It is imperative that the individual know at the onset of this assignment exactly what power is associated with the assignment. Such topics as what decisions the leader wants to be included in and what decisions the employee can make, should be addressed. If there are others involved who have decision-making authority in this project, that information should be shared as well.

What parameters exist with this assignment?

In considering parameters, address issues such as how much freedom the individual has to be creative in problem solving or in developing enhancements to the project. Clearly communicate whether thinking outside the box is an option or if instructions are to be followed exactly as stated.

35

Nancy Mercurio

*Are there other individuals working on this or
something similar?*

Ensure alignment occurs wherever possible, making every
attempt to minimize duplication of efforts and wasted time
and energy. Disclose any information available regarding other individuals or groups currently working on this
concept or those who may have previously worked on the
concept. If there is previous history that should be considered, point the individual in the right direction.

*What resources are available; financial, human,
materials?*

Some projects require purchases, which may include
services or materials. This information should be communicated to the individual selected prior to the onset
of activities. It is also important to disclose additional
headcount that may be accessible if help is needed.

*Which areas of this assignment do you need to
participate in?*

Some leaders do an excellent job of clarifying parameters for their participation when delegating, but then
insert themselves into the process more than what was
initially communicated. While unexpected involvement
may be justified, the value of the experience to the individual is likely to be compromised.

Frequent insertion, even when necessary, can easily be
mistaken for micromanagement, and will inevitably minimize the empowerment associated with delegation.

It is best to delegate with less authority and fewer parameters, slowly increasing the level of independence as the
individual proves worthy of the responsibility assigned.
This approach actually maximizes empowerment to the
individual and optimizes results.

Risk factors must be considered when anticipating your level of participation. Such factors may include the need for high-level visibility due to project business impact, the value in knowledge sharing, and any risks to the individual based upon lack of ability or knowledge. If the initiative is highly visible to the entire organization, then you will want to maintain a more active role. Conversely, less visible projects will require less involvement on your part and must be stated as such. Individuals with less experience who are being given the chance to expand their knowledge will need greater oversight than those more experienced.

Communicating exactly what role you want to play is the point, regardless of what level of involvement there is. Doing so eliminates speculation about your participation and eliminates frustration and corrective actions.

MAINTAINING CONSISTENT PRACTICES

Once you have determined and communicated your preference for involvement, the next step is to ensure that you maintain predictable and consistent practices. Adhering to consistency will minimize conflict and prevent you from being seen as a leader who assigns responsibility without authority.

A leader's image and credibility are always at risk when actions do not align with words. Allowing an employee to perceive he or she has autonomy that virtually does not exist, can have lasting damage on both the leader and the individual.

Nancy Mercurio

The best safeguard in this case is to act in concert with your communicated plan; no more, no less. If you initially stated that weekly meetings would be held, then hold weekly meetings. If you issued authority to someone else during the delegation process, then adhere to the agreement and act accordingly unless challenges occur. When changes are necessary, communicate clearly the intention. No surprises.

The foundation for appraising one's credibility is derived from the perspective that words and actions are predictable and trustworthy. As a leader, you must hold yourself accountable to acting as intended. Any deviations should be communicated openly and in all cases, prior to taking action. Once trust has been broken, it becomes an insurmountable task to change perspective; regardless of the effort applied. Any subsequent actions will automatically be considered suspect.

When is the desired completion date or time?

Be sure to clearly state the expected, non-negotiable completion date; the date that the entire project is approved, completed, and available for use or delivery. The completion date is not the date that the project gets reviewed or receives additional approvals, and this information must be clearly communicated upfront.

Assuming your actions and words are aligned overall, the next step is in knowing how to manage the unexpected; situations where inserting your input is necessary. Your ability to handle such challenges will determine how smoothly adjustments are implemented, and how effective individuals are in executing required changes.

GAIN PERSPECTIVE BEFORE MAKING ADJUSTMENTS

There are many factors that contribute to your ability to gain perspective before making adjustments. First, it is important to speak with anyone closely aligned to the activity; particularly those in charge. The goal is to ensure you have access to those who can provide the greatest insight into the current situation; those with the most exposure.

Next, it is necessary to mitigate risks related to your involvement at this point. Any adjustment will have an affect or pose a threat and therefore, must be carefully evaluated. Evaluating risks related to making adjustments should be conducted in a collaborative manner to ensure success.

Gaining objectivity is also important in these situations. As a leader, your role requires *taking the elevator up* high enough to have the greatest overview of the situation. Operating at the detailed level everyone else does will add zero value in determining the best course of action.

The goal at this point is to rise above the situation and gain a leadership perspective. Remaining neutral is a key factor. When you can be completely impartial, you'll find it far easier to identify those who are overly passionate, or too attached to a specific outcome. From this advantage point, you can recognize the person or persons who can drive the adjustments with minimal risk to the project or initiative.

Timing has an impact on your ability to gain perspective as well. If you make adjustments without careful consideration of all elements, there is likely to be an increased risk for failure. Give your undivided attention to the situation, consider all the facts, and weigh in on the final plan for moving forward with adjustments before any actions are taken. Behaving in a conscious and intended manner will eliminate potential problems and preserve your energy for the more important work at hand.

When focused on driving the organization's mission, delegating is often more about *how to accomplish the challenges at hand, rather than who can deliver the best results.* However, the value in selecting the right person for the task cannot be overlooked. Equally important to consider is who would benefit most from the assignment from a growth and development perspective.

MATCHING TALENTS TO TASKS

New responsibilities or assignments can be reenergizing for those who have become stagnant in their routine duties, and can reinforce positive behaviors in those who continue to seek opportunities for growth.

Being selected for a new assignment sends a message of value to the employee. Given *perception is reality,* employees who perceive themselves as worthy, typically contribute their worth.

Finding the best person for the job should include consideration of each of the following:

- What professional growth opportunities exist?

- What skills will be utilized and/or can be improved upon?

- When risks are mitigated, which individuals are best suited?

- Who could benefit most from this opportunity?

- What flexibility is required if any, and who demonstrates the flexibility needed?

- Does a mentoring opportunity exist and if so, for whom?

One of the biggest mistakes many leaders make in delegating is to select according to *who will require the least amount of oversight*; even when it means selecting the same individual repeatedly. In some cases, it is a matter of having experience with particular individuals in similar initiatives and confidence in their ability to deliver results. In other cases, the inability to spend additional time managing the project may be the sole reason for choosing the same individual each time. However, without some investment in those employees less noticeable, only a small percentage of your team's talents are leveraged. Contributions from the same individuals will emerge the same year after year; making performance review discussions seem more like *Ground Hog Day.*

No doubt, it will require substantially more time to establish the practice of conducting a more thorough assessment prior to delegation. Yet, the long-term results can be beneficial as increased growth and development leads to improved overall output. While the path of least resistance is often preferred, the choice to develop more than the select few on your team who show potential, will lead to greater output collectively.

Acting in accordance with your communicated plans eliminates potential problems and most importantly will add to your credibility as a leader. Equally important, doing so will increase personal self-worth, improving overall output while capitalizing on the talent you have hired.

Delegating responsibly and providing clarity around all facets of the delegation at the time of the assignment will produce the best results and minimize unnecessary efforts.

CHAPTER 5

Perspective and Communication

Gaining perspective in every situation requires having the ability to communicate effectively, listen without judgment, and decode underlying messages in every exchange. Using communication to ensure clarity before taking action is the key to effectively managing the environment. However, the challenge lies in learning how to become an effective communicator.

Millions of dollars are expended each year on training programs related to effective communication, all intended to improve business efficiency and increase productivity. Most leaders have taken at least two formal classes in their career, if not more, and all have had ample practical experience that produced both positive and negative results. Yet, in spite of the investment of time and dollars to improve communications in the workplace, many leaders find themselves struggling to get employees to complete assigned work as expected. Why?

The reason is really quite simple. Leadership requires the ability to thoroughly evaluate a situation and the people involved before actions are taken. Doing so requires full comprehension of existing facts surrounding the situation as well as the perspectives of those driving the process. Reality and perspective are not always synonymous; however addressing both is what propels the situation into forward motion.

Nancy Mercurio

Moving a person or issue forward can only occur when the individual's perception of the situation is understood. Therefore, the leader must possess the ability to fully interpret the perspective the individual has related to the assigned work. It is also imperative for the leader to recognize that individual perception can be a huge point of contention.

To avoid constant frustration, a leader must be willing to embrace the fact that

Perspective = Reality!

No matter how ridiculous the interpretation, *perspective is reality* for anyone involved. Addressing and shifting a person's reality is as valuable as providing solutions.

Not all leaders subscribe to this belief and many push their agendas in spite of the perceptions of those involved. In fact, some leaders will actually repeat their message the exact same way multiple times in an attempt to get others to align with their views. This practice is almost as comical as watching a person who over-enunciates and shouts when engaged in conversations where a language barrier exists!

Focusing on driving your own points in spite of how others feel is ineffective and does little to gain buy-in. Addressing perspective first will gain support for the work that must be accomplished, require less management oversight and improve overall outcomes. It all boils down to having the ability to communicate specifically to the needs of the current situation.

Whether managing home, work or global issues, lack of understanding and differences in opinions have fueled conflicts for centuries. In most situations, it is improbable that two people will view a situation in exactly the same manner because neither have had *exactly* the same experiences. It is virtually impossible to capture an image of one's thoughts or the thought process itself, including how they arrive at conclusions. As a result, differing views are inevitable whenever two or more people are involved.

The art of moving people past their views requires gaining perspective and communicating effectively. Differences must be evaluated based upon intentions, not words. People tend to become fixated on *who said what,* but fail to discuss *what was intended,* or *interpreted as intended* meaning. Once a situation reaches the point of differing opinions, discussing who said what only increases dissention. The quickest means of resolving differences is to evaluate the gap between what is intended and what is perceived as intended.

The example below provides some clarity around this point:

> During a regularly scheduled staff meeting, you tell the team about a phone call you received earlier that same day. The call was in regards to a project your team is working on.

> You want to share the information in an objective and factual manner without indicating you have formed an opinion one way or the other. Additionally, you are hoping to avoid any interruption to the team's momentum or negate their efforts.

Nancy Mercurio

The approach you take is as follows:

Margaret Smith phoned earlier today and shared that her team is having some challenges related to Project A. It would be good to get our project leaders dialoguing with her team to resolve any concerns.

The nodding of heads confirms you are heard and no further discussion ensues.

Three days later, you receive a second call from Margaret, again sharing her concerns related to Project A. You ask if she had received a call from any of the project leads to which she replies no. Within seconds, you have formed an opinion and you perceive the team ignored your request because you took a softer, less demanding approach.

Immediately upon ending the call, you email the team asking the project leaders why they failed to contact Margaret's team after you had made the request at the meeting earlier in the week. Additionally, you direct them to decide who is making the call and to get back to you as soon as the call is completed.

One of the team leaders replies to all with the following message:

While I do recall you mentioning Margaret at the meeting, I don't believe any of us walked away thinking that it was necessary to have a conversation with her, or her team before our weekly project call this Friday. Her team participates in the call and it seemed a fitting time to raise the concern.

Now here's where the situation goes from bad to worse. Like many leaders, you decided to reply to the email defending yourself with the following statements:

- *I communicated the problem and hoped the group would take the hint.*

- *Why would I have mentioned it if I didn't want you to take action now?*

- *I didn't think I had to spell it out for individuals at this level.*

Taking a defensive position in this scenario does nothing more than add to the problem and encourage another round of email exchanges without moving the situation forward.

A more effective response would be one of the following:

- *Good point. I forgot about the weekly meeting. Can you call her now?*

- *I can see why you thought that. Can you call her today?*

- *My mistake, but please call her today and get back to me.*

These three sample responses are simple replies that require little effort to create, yet are unlikely first choices in similar situations. The more common practice is to defend one's perspective and respond with less favorable, unproductive comments and there are several reasons why:

When leaders perceive they are being ignored or that the direction they have provided is not considered a priority, remaining objective can be very challenging. No one likes to feel disrespected and the frustration that develops can be overwhelming.

Sometimes, the need to be right outweighs the desire to resolve the situation and move on. In every case, regardless of the details, it is always too late to worry about what happened.

In some cases, defensive reactions are simply a matter of pride and ego-based thinking; *I'll show them who is boss*; or *Margaret thinks I am a poor leader,* or *I wonder who else has heard about these issues by now.*

Regardless of the cause for responding defensively, it is a useless practice that creates additional problems, requires corrective actions, and is flat out exhausting. Give it up!

Let go of defensive practices, as they will never serve you well!

Communicating before gaining perspective is a huge mistake and the damage is often irreversible. There is no means of erasing what has already been said and heard or the interpretation of those words.

In the example of Margaret Smith, continuing a dialogue around what you think was said in the meeting or why others should have known better, will not address Margaret's concerns. Further discussion at this point is as effective as five people standing around a derailed train scratching their heads trying to figure out what happened. Meanwhile, there is a shipment on the derailed train that is now delayed from reaching its destination.

Getting the team back on track is the leader's job and should remain the top priority.

The goal in these situations should be to focus your attention on achieving resolution and evaluating lessons learned to ensure a similar situation in the future can be avoided. Resolving such differences requires centering one's attention on how to regain momentum and minimize down time, regardless of what was said or done.

In business, everything from hiring decisions to goals and objectives is dependent upon the leader's ability to evaluate what is needed (gain perspective), communicate intentions or desired outcomes, and guide all subsequent activities accordingly. While there is no magical formula for success, some common sense principles can be incorporated into everyday practices as outlined below:

SIMPLIFY COMMUNICATIONS

Whether communicating in person, via phone or through email, communication must be simple and clear in order to drive the points. While it is important to share knowledge, education, and experience in ways that demonstrate the value you bring to the organization, communication that is overstated can be intimidating.

For example, in-group settings where the leader speaks eloquently or uses complicated terminology, many people are uncomfortable raising their hands when prompted for questions on the topic. While there are likely many unanswered questions in the room, few will exude the same level of confidence as the speaker.

When communication is simplified, it invites greater participation, which leads to a leader's improved understanding of the environment and/or the subject at hand. Whether intentional or unintentional, establishing distance between you and your audience is without value and usually requires additional explanations.

Nancy Mercurio

Speaking in simple and easy to comprehend terms will capture attention regardless of the methodology used to convey the message. While it is valuable for each of us to expand our vocabulary, large and impressive words are best utilized in one-on-one conversations with individuals of matching interests and skills. Maintaining simplicity overall will keep people engaged and improve the potential for a successful outcome.

Employees respect leaders who help them feel comfortable while in their presence. That comfort level leads to greater interest in organizational objectives and allows for improved outcomes.

The easiest way to simplify a message is to apply the basic skills you learned in elementary school when composing your first story or book report. It's a concept we can all easily recall: Intro, Topic, and Conclusion:

Intro
Describe the purpose for the meeting or communication.

Topic
Discuss the issue or need and expectations related to who, what, where and how.

Conclusion
Explain next steps or any follow-up required.

This approach can be applied to the most complex topics and still serve as the quickest route to providing clarity-surrounding tasks. Whether in-person, via phone or via email, remember to keep it simple.

50

Remain Focused

It's easy to divert from the agenda when passionate about a topic. We have all experienced meetings where the person speaking slowly migrates away from the specific agenda item, losing audience interest in the process. When audience members lose interest, people start to doodle, check email, or send text messages on their mobile devices.

While it is important to share one's passion and experience related to a particular subject, communicating with clarity should always be the primary goal.

Leave Nothing to Interpretation

The majority of gossip in the workplace is about perception and unknown factors, rather than facts. Implied messages that lack clarity leave people speculating about intentions, and speculation leads to unproductive conversations, which ultimately distracts from accomplishing work. Imagine the boring conversations that would take place around the water cooler if facts were the only topic discussed!

Given human interest in speculation, a leader must over communicate expectations and clarify parameters surrounding those expectations, in order to maximize productivity.

Whether leaving a voicemail, writing an email, or delivering a message face-to-face, *say what you mean and mean what you say*; leaving nothing to interpretation.

To eliminate speculation and avoid misinterpretation, incorporate the following guidelines into your daily practices:

- If actions are required clarify what, who, and when.

- If a specific person is intended to hear your message, use their name.

- If you want two people to work together on something, name them.

- If you are inviting questions, ask what questions you can answer.

- If you need a response to a request, state by when.

- If you need a task completed today, don't say, 'when you get a chance'.

- If you are upset, tell the people you are upset with; not their colleagues.

- If you need an hour of someone's time, don't ask for a few minutes.

Some leaders prefer to communicate less information initially. Doing so will only later elicit a barrage of questions as the various unknowns emerge; all of which will eventually have to be communicated to everyone to ensure consistency. The amount of time required for clarification can be better spent serving business and organizational needs. Anything less than clear and concise communication leaves the impression that the leader was unprepared or unable to fully evaluate all factors prior to the initial communication.

While it is certainly not suggested that you burden or bore others with mounds of details, the goal is to provide clear communication at all times and leave nothing to interpretation.

OPEN AND HONEST COMMUNICATION

Practically every organization boasts of having a core value related to open and honest communication. Beyond words however, there is little meaning to the value unless incorporated into daily practices. In spite of elaborate attempts to address open and honest communication, employees still only trust those they perceive as having their best interest at heart.

In some cases where leaders have expressed genuine interest in the well-being of their employees and intent is pure, there are still those who do not trust. This can be a result of a previous boss or relationship and have little or nothing to do with the current leader.

While you cannot control the thoughts or actions of another, you can improve your side of the equation by acting in a trusting manner. Doing so requires fully managing your role in communications; demonstrating integrity at all times.

It is also your responsibility to invite integrity from others; creating an environment that is conducive to sharing differences of opinion without fear of defensive reactions or repercussions. Establishing the practice of open and honest communications is important. When you have reasons to suspect that truthful communications are not occurring, it is your job as a leader to address the suspicion in a timely manner.

Be mindful of ways to provide guidance for improved communications. For example, if a direct report speaks to you about a colleague, your first obligation is to guide the individual to work through the challenge with the colleague, not to intervene. If the individual cannot share their concerns with the person involved, offer to mediate with both parties present. Do not offer to communicate the problem on behalf of the individual because once you do, you will have invited this as a continued practice. Moreover, in doing so, you minimize opportunity for improved communications between the parties involved.

Cultural differences can prevent open and honest communication. Some cultures practice non-confrontational communication, while other cultures do not approve of openly sharing views. In these situations, individuals will share their views when prompted but will often speak only in general terms. More effort on your part to invite additional dialogue will eventually lead to improved, forthright communications.

Another way to encourage open communications is to avoid engaging in conversations related to second-hand information. For example, when someone informs you that they overheard a conversation where you were the unpopular topic, do not react or respond. Simply ask the individual sharing this information to encourage people to speak to you directly. Thank the individual for their concern and move on.

By not responding, you discourage the continued practice of sharing second hand information and instead, encourage the practice of holding others accountable to open and honest communication.

Your role is to set the example by ensuring that your actions and efforts promote an environment that supports truthful exchanges.

LISTEN FOR PERSPECTIVE

In leadership, listening is a key component in uncovering the perspective of others. Many people lack the communication skills needed to share their thoughts or find the right words to explain the situation. Through listening to the core message being conveyed, you can help decipher the message.

Avoid judgment of how the message is being communicated and listen carefully for a common theme or concept to emerge. There is risk associated with sharing the truth. For example, few employees will ever approach a leader and admit to being in over their head on a project or unable to perform as expected. Often times, an employee is apprehensive to admit shortcomings due to concerns that the situation might not be viewed as an isolated incident or as being project related.

To gain perspective through listening, avoid judging what is being shared. Focus your attention instead on the individual's perception of the problem and ways you can assist. Don't allow feelings to overrule your thoughts. In spite of how ridiculous the situation may sound to you, it is very real to the individual experiencing it.

For example:

> Imagine a situation where the employee is trying to gain your guidance without sharing the specific challenge. The conversation is somewhat generic; however, you suspect there is more to the story. If you listen only to the words, you could end up listening for an hour without ever learning what guidance is needed. Conversely, if you listen intently for the underlying concerns, you can quickly determine how to assist.

55

Nancy Mercurio

Consider the following scenario:

> John comes to your office and says, *Boy, customer service metrics can be a tough process. One piece of incorrect information can quickly lead to an entire set of facts and figures being off.*

If you merely concur with John on the topic of metrics data collection and he's in need of help, this conversation will be one of sharing experiences only. However, if you pay closer attention, you'll quickly deduce that John might be facing a challenge in the gathering of metrics needed for the upcoming meeting. Your job is to gain perspective and uncover the need as follows:

> *John, are we speaking in general terms here or did you run into a snag with the metrics you are gathering for the meeting? If you need any help, I'm happy to assist.*

Once you open the door for John to be honest, he is far more likely to reach out if he is struggling. Most importantly, you have sent a clear message to John that you are willing to help in future situations. Paying attention to the hidden message is the key to providing proper guidance in these situations.

ASK QUESTIONS

The most effective means of uncovering the intended message in any communication is to ask a series of questions. When you ask questions, it allows the other person the chance to hear how the message is being perceived. Hearing the message reflected back provides an opportunity to confirm or adjust the communication accordingly. Asking questions closes the gap between the message being conveyed and the message being heard.

This method for providing feedback minimizes risk associated with eliciting emotions or defensive responses, particularly in a heated or controversial discussion. When you ask questions, the receiver is forced to focus on the question being asked and not the person speaking. Whereas in conventional feedback, the receiver focuses more on the person and the tone in which the message is conveyed.

When using this questioning feedback method, it is critical that you maintain a neutral and inviting tone. Any hint of sarcasm or hidden meaning will negate the communicator and ultimately lead to a negative exchange.

Consider the following questions as examples of this point:

Negative tone
How is it possible you didn't receive the memo?

Preferred question
Are you saying you didn't receive the memo?

Negative tone
Do you mean no one helped you?

Preferred question
So you didn't get the help you needed?

If you read the questions above aloud, you can hear the difference between the negative tone and the preferred questions. You can also imagine the type of response you would receive when asking questions with the negative tone.

While there are other methods for providing feedback, conveying the message through a series of questions is the least intimidating and can help to ease tension.

Avoid using the parroting style of feedback where the listener recites almost verbatim what was heard. Most of us have been on the receiving end of someone who uses this approach and nothing is more irritating. This approach can also ignite a disagreement during a heated exchange and decrease any chance for resolution.

Asking questions can help you quickly ascertain the problem and move towards a solution. It is a targeted approach, which is known to produce targeted responses.

Gaining perspective in communication is one of the more difficult tasks a leader faces. Communications are required in all aspects of daily activities and can positively or negatively impact business outcomes.

Ensuring communications are clear requires the ability to elevate yourself; rising above what is being said to uncover what is needed. When you invest time to clarify perspective and needs, you will ultimately improve efficiency, effectiveness, and output.

CHAPTER 6

Coaching with Improved Objectivity

There are other ways to improve individual and organizational effectiveness, such as through coaching. This critical aspect of the leader's role is the art of cultivating behaviors in others to help them achieve desired outcomes through providing sage guidance. The process requires the ability to be objective in assisting others to reach their full potential through a realistic assessment of facts, interests, ability, and output. Personal desires for the individual, as well as judgment of actions must be set aside in order to keep the individual's best interest at the forefront of all efforts. Through one-on-one listening, advising and training, the leader as *Coach,* can become fully invested in the well-being of another person; while at the same time identifying realistic paths for individual and career development.

The coaching process is best described as *leveraging talents*; finding ways to maximize the investment you made when hiring these specific employees. Most organizations under utilize employee capacity which defeats the purpose of hiring qualified people in the first place. The goal is to find ways to hone skills in each individual that capitalizes on strengths and stretches them to new heights of performance. The individual benefits as much as the organization through growth and development and often gains skills that reach far beyond behaviors alone. Through the coaching process, many employees learn life skills such as improved cognitive development, political savvy and the value of collaborative efforts.

Every leader should find ways to showcase each individual's talents and benefit from this collective wealth of knowledge and skills in the organization. The greatest gift to the individual and the organization is in maximizing performance.

The role of *Coach* requires establishing mutual trust and demonstrating integrity in all communications. Little growth can occur if an individual does not perceive that he or she can completely and unequivocally depend upon truthfulness and support from the leader, even when mistakes are made.

This is one of the most honoring and valuable contributions the leader can make as it will have a lasting impact on someone's future. Each of us remembers a teacher or person who coached us in some form or another during our early years while in school or pursuing hobbies. The words spoken and the lessons learned possessed lifetime value and regardless of our age, we can still recall the experience.

Recollection likely also includes coaching experiences that caused grave damage to our psyche, impacting our confidence to achieve in specific areas. Coaches more interested in the 'win' than the player have been known to cause experiences of public humiliation. Such behaviors have prevented many individuals from continuing to pursue their interests.

Some leaders have had a similar impact on their employees by identifying and discussing weaknesses more than strengths, and through constant comparison of one employee to another or to themselves. Stories of how the leader climbed the ladder or their ability to with-stand the pressure often serve as a de-motivator to the individual struggling to succeed. Such practices must not be misconstrued as coaching efforts, as they are devoid of true interest in the achievements of another based upon capacity. Clearly one person's ability to realize full potential pales in comparison to another without independent consideration of individual capabil-ity, and capacity for learning.

Each day in every organization, there are leaders who either help employees to stretch their skills or to feel incompetent. With one statement, one compliment, or one disapproving look, the employee shines or withdraws. It is a huge responsibility for leaders and requires conscious thought regarding the impact of what is about to be said or done. While there are some leaders who enjoy a bit of chest puffing and power mongering, negative impact to the employee is usually a result of lack of patience or time to nurture individuals through challenging situations. This is one of the reasons many organizations today have resorted to hiring external coaches to assist employees.

When individuals are contributing value but need per-sonal training or guidance to improve overall, or when an individual is targeted for growth, seeking external help can be more effective.

Another reason for seeking external coaching is that it can be difficult for the leader to remain fully objective when guiding an individual. This is especially true in situations where the leader must coach a long-term employee. However, it is important to note that investing time in fully developing one employee without being able to do the same for another is easily misinterpreted as favoritism.

Nancy Mercurio

Although there are definitely times when hiring an external coach is in the best interest of both the leader and the employee, there are many ways in which the leader can provide coaching on a daily basis to all employees.

Understanding the coaching process can be simplified when comparing the role of business leader to sports coach. There are many commonalities between these two roles and business leaders can benefit from taking the sports coach approach.

In sports, the goal is to develop a strategy to execute collaborative efforts that will achieve the objective. Strategic planning encompasses taking the best approach to the task at hand, coupled with identifying those who will be the most effective in carrying out the mission.

The strategy is communicated prior to and during the game, and players receive ongoing, individual and group guidance. Using a combination of words, cryptic hand gestures and facial expressions, the coach is fully able to guide the execution of the desired strategy.

There are several factors that make the sports coach a successful leader:

1. The coach thoroughly studies and understands the behaviors of key players.
2. Developing a strategy always includes efforts to leverage player capability.
3. At no time during the game does the coach execute a play.
4. Personal observation is the sole source for identifying problems.
5. Feedback or guidance provided is always timely.

For the sports coach, a winning strategy is only possible through identifying strengths and weaknesses on the team and matching talents to tasks. Emphasis placed on which individuals are best suited to deliver the objective is indeed the most significant difference between business and sports coaching. In sports, the strategy is designed with player capability as the primary focus. Beyond the overall objective of winning the game, every strategic plan is centered on who will do what to achieve the goal.

In the workplace, strategic discussions at the executive level rarely focus on who will carry out duties. While it usually known who the targeted group or department is, focus at this point is typically on developing the most successful business strategy. Individual capacity is often assessed at the implementation versus strategy stage. The leader responsible for executing the strategy is the one responsible for determining who is best suited for the mission through evaluation of past performance, skill set, and ability to deliver under pressure (Delegation-Chapter 4).

Feedback is another area in which the business leader and sports coach differ in approach. In a sports game, the coach provides feedback immediately following each play. Players are reminded of the goal at each opportunity along the way, and are prepared for the obstacles ahead.

In the workplace however, feedback is provided when employees seek help or obstacles have already occurred. In some cases, feedback may be as much as days later if challenges are saved for update meetings. This can create a problem particularly in situations where there is a behavioral issue, as feedback shared in a timely manner is more useful. Less timely feedback places more reliance on individual, subjective memory.

Although existing differences in approaches are understandable, there are indeed benefits that leaders can glean from the sports coach such as:

- Placing more emphasis on individual growth and development;

- Recognizing that the individual player is as important as the strategy;

- Preparing individuals for the obstacles ahead;

- Providing more timely feedback;

- Focusing attention on leveraging individual talents to capitalize on the investment.

Football is an aspect of sports that can also be valuable in driving understanding of the coaching role at work. In football games, there is a primary *Coach* and a *Quarterback* who must work together closely to deliver the objectives of the game. The workplace is quite similar in that there is typically a leader responsible for the objective and a project lead assigned to carry out the mission. Some leaders try to act as both which diminishes any sub-leader roles and can appear as micromanagement.

At the onset of projects or major activities, the leader must decide whether he or she is playing the role of *Coach* or *Quarterback*. The difference is quite simple:

As Coach, the leader works closely with the project lead on strategy and goals, and allows the project lead to help drive the tasks.

As Quarterback, the leader is involved in actually helping carry out the details of the mission.

To be effective, you must identify the role you want to play, communicate your intentions, and avoid deviating from the plan.

Using this model, you can easily monitor your efforts and take the necessary steps to correct your actions when the divisional lines become muddled.

There are a variety of factors that determine the effectiveness of the coaching process, and when incorporated, will optimize individual contribution.

COACHING AND OBJECTIVITY

In coaching, being objective is an essential ingredient that determines the difference between success and failure. Providing guidance that cultivates improved behaviors in another person requires the ability to identify the gap between current reality and desired outcomes; *the difference between individual capability and the skills identified to drive organizational success.* Sounds simple in theory, but in actuality requires thoughtful and objective perspective.

Assessing individual capability should include observation of the following:

Role effectiveness, communication skills, ability to handle conflict, successes and challenges in performance to date; skills demonstrated beyond expectation; skills that fall short of expectation; best and poorest performance observed.

An objective perspective of individual capability is the key.

Nancy Mercurio

COMMUNICATION IN COACHING

The first and most important step in the coaching relationship is to ensure both you and the individual agree on the current reality of existing behaviors; what the individual is doing or not doing, the impact of those behaviors, what the individual would like to be (or should be) doing; and the impact of improved behaviors. If there is disagreement on current reality, the coaching process will be ineffective. Ensuring you both agree on current reality is the best place to start.

Clear communication is the fundamental component necessary to drive improved behaviors.

Some questions to ask in uncovering the individual's perspective include:

- What do you believe to be your strengths in this role?

- How have those strengths positively impacted the organization?

- What behaviors are considered shortcomings?

- Can you describe your best performance to date in this role?

- What do you consider to be your poorest performance?

- How do your current behaviors align with expectations?

Asking questions is the fastest way to achieve a starting point and certainly the most effective means of driving improvements. The answers to each of these questions will provide you with valuable insights and lead you to a point where you can begin providing guidance.

Always allow the individual to share their perspective before sharing yours. Leaders are often too quick to provide their assessments of a situation before uncovering the individual's perspective. When you provide your insights first, there is a 50% chance that the individual might not share your perspective, which means wasting your time and theirs. In addition, some individuals who hear your perspective first will be hesitant to share their own, especially when it differs from yours.

Allowing the individual to share first is risk free and immediately helps you attain the information you need. Your opinion at this point has less value and will do little to shift behaviors in another person. Once you understand the individual's perspective, you can concur or disagree and move forward from there.

Through your communication skills, you can guide the self-discovery process, which is one of the most valuable experiences in coaching. Self-discovery is the quickest pathway to improvement and empowerment. Your job as a coach is to utilize your communication skills to gain insight into the situation through the individual's perspective, offering guidance where needed.

DESIRE TO IMPROVE

Individual desire to improve must be established before you can assist another person in growing and developing. Nothing you say or do will improve the behaviors of another unless they are a willing participant and perceive the value. The individual must be willing to invest the time and effort necessary to drive the improvements and commit to the coaching process, which means being receptive to feedback.

Questions to uncover an individual's desire to improve:

- Do you agree changes are needed to improve your abilities?

- Are you willing to do the work it takes to get there?

- Are you open to receiving feedback and guidance during the process?

Individual commitment is essential for success, and the commitment must be verbalized before the coaching process begins.

IDENTIFYING AREAS FOR DEVELOPMENT

Once the desire to improve is validated, it is time to identify areas of focus for growth and development efforts. It is best to target those behaviors that will have the greatest impact if improved. One behavioral change can positively impact several areas within the role. Isolating areas for improvement versus trying to fix all deficiencies at once is the best approach.

Targeted behaviors should also be those that are utilized in existing work or current activities to maximize value to the individual. Little value will emerge from coaching an individual on a behavior that has a small impact on the role overall. Increased opportunity for application of skills will lead to success in driving newly acquired behaviors.

Circumstances may dictate areas of focus for development:

If a challenging situation has arisen and immediate corrective actions are needed, then coaching should be focused on improving the situation.

If an individual has recently underperformed, coaching efforts should focus on shortcomings.

If the individual is targeted for growth within the organization and improvements would enhance visibility, areas of focus should be on those behaviors that will have the greatest impact.

In all three scenarios, the individual must be able to identify and comprehend the downfalls of their current behaviors and see value in investing time and effort to improve.

Once the areas of focus have been identified, desired behaviors should be documented as goals with brief explanations as in the example below:

Goal—Improve efficiency with data management

Eliminate hand written documents and learn to use appropriate software for all data management.

Progress on goals can be tracked in a simple spreadsheet created by the leader and preferably managed by the individual. Each of you should retain a copy of all goals for easy reference and for use during follow-up discussions.

Nancy Mercurio

PROVIDING GUIDANCE

The easiest way to begin the process of providing guidance is to restate what was agreed to as a starting point; revisiting each of the objectives for the coaching process. Ask questions for clarity as outlined in the example below:

Example Discussion:

> Sue, as we agreed, improving your efficiency in managing data is a targeted goal for improvement. Having you use company-selected software exclusively to record information by the end of the quarter will eliminate extra steps, help you stay organized, and make the information more readily accessible to everyone else who needs it.
>
> The question is how do we achieve the desired outcome? What thoughts do you have on getting started and how can I help?

At this point, your role is to serve as the guiding light in helping the individual achieve the best possible approach, rather than be the answer provider. In most situations, the individual is capable of identifying next steps, but is simply too close to the situation to gain perspective. That's where you come in. Your job is to ask questions that help put things into perspective.

Take the Elevator Up & Take the Individual With You!

> Let's say Sue decides that one approach would be to remove all the paper from her desk, which she believes would then force her to use the designated software instead.

While you understand her thought process, you believe it is completely impossible for her to work paperless during the day. You have observed her office and know the amount of papers that are piled up on her desk; many of which contain her handwriting all over them.

It would be easy to send Sue a clear message through a facial expression as to how ridiculous you think the idea is. Alternatively, you could act as the guiding light and ask: *what do you currently use paper for*? Asking the question would help her quickly identify how unrealistic the idea actually is.

While this question and answer process may be extremely tedious and time consuming, investing time upfront to drive self-discovery will lead to learning. Revisiting the problem repeatedly over months or even years is far more time consuming and behaviors remain unchanged. Your willingness to lead the student to the lesson is a long-term investment and will drive improvements.

In every case, whether an ongoing effort or spur of the moment coaching opportunity, providing guidance should encompass the self-discovery process when possible. Not including the self-discovery component will lead to repeating the experience rather than ensuring a lesson is learned.

Understanding the value of not being an answer provider is vital to the coaching process. It may seem senseless to possess the experience and wisdom to be the *Coach,* yet not be able to share that knowledge in a more open manner. However, the goal is to utilize your expertise to create an experience in which learning can occur, offering your sage advice in the right and perfect moments.

Nancy Mercurio

Coaching is about facilitating learning in another, sharing your insights when the person asks, identifying inconsistencies, or asking questions that address possible risks. Equally important is recognizing patterns of behavior that the individual simply can't distinguish on their own. Think of it like a science class where every experiment is guided by the teacher but the work is completed by the student.

LISTENING

As you can already see, listening is an important component of coaching. While observation is a valuable asset during the coaching process, listening is the most effective means of gaining the individual's perspective. Through listening, you can identify the challenge being faced and possibly prevent a repeat performance of an ineffective practice. In critical moments, listening is how you identify what guidance is needed.

Timing is an important component in listening while coaching. When you don't have time to stop and listen, you should acknowledge the fact rather than risk appearing disinterested. To the receiver, partial listening signals a lack of interest and can affect the relationship. Sending emails, taking phone calls or completing paperwork while someone is speaking to you are all indicators that you are not fully listening. If timing is bad, identify a better time for the discussion, but avoid appearing as a disinterested coach. With repeated occurrences, the individual will equate your lack of attention to a lack of interest in wanting to help. With this perception, the value of the guidance is minimized and the process becomes ineffective.

In face-to-face discussions, eye contact implies intent to listen. Pay attention and focus on the individual. If helpful, repeat their words silently to yourself as they speak to assist you in remaining engaged in the conversation.

72

COACHING VIA PHONE

Listening is also the most critical factor in conducting coaching via phone. When listening attentively, you can actually learn more than you might if the conversation were held in person where it is easy to become distracted by facial expressions and behaviors. Giving full attention to the individual while taking strategic notes will help you quickly uncover the problems and guide the individual to solutions. When the approach begins to sound as though it is headed in a direction that will unlikely be effective, you can interject and ask more questions.

When conducting coaching remotely via phone, listening will aid you in knowing when the individual has become distracted. Your job as a *Coach* is to stop talking during times when the individual does not appear to be listening, and ask questions such as *do you need a minute or is this a bad time to continue?* Above all, do not ignore any change in tone or obvious distractions during the conversation. Doing so is a waste of time.

In any phone discussion, be sure to eliminate distractions on your end such as open email. Turn your monitor off and place your mobile phone on silent. Giving your undivided attention to the individual will eliminate having to repeat the discussion or revisit the experience.

COACHING VIA EMAIL

Coaching can also be accomplished through email exchanges. Asking for insights or clarity on a situation via email provides a documented exchange of the issue, which you can retain and revisit as needed to compare patterns of behavior. The email approach eliminates having to rely on memory for all recollection of the individual's thoughts and behaviors. Plus, each time you read and review the email, you will have additional insights into the individual's behaviors.

Nancy Mercurio

Through emailing a few simple questions, you can make a quick assessment of the situation and evaluate the individual's thoughts. This approach especially works well in environments where the individual you are coaching is not visible to you on a daily basis.

Coaching is a valuable service in the leader's role and requires strength in being objective in all aspects of the coaching process. Clarifying the role you will play, monitoring yourself to ensure words and actions are aligned, and demonstrating full interest in the individual, will create a trusting and valuable relationship. When trust exists, you can assist in developing an individual's capabilities beyond expectation and everyone benefits from the process.

Coaching is an integral part of leadership. Investing time and energy in others can have the biggest impact on their career, on yours, and on the organization!

CHAPTER 7

Driving Organizational Perspective

For most leaders, the responsibility of overseeing daily activities can be daunting, leaving little time to strategize and even less time to communicate the strategy. Meetings, troubleshooting, and constant interruptions make it difficult for leaders to find time for connecting the dots between daily activities and organizational strategy. As a result, employees tend to busy themselves more with the details of the tasks they perform, often unaware of how their contributions align with organizational objectives. In fact, there are many employees who have spent years working for an organization without being able to articulate how the job they perform actually contributes to the organization's success. Although it is the leader's responsibility to address strategy and goals, the employee should be equally responsible for seeking this information. Unfortunately, daily tasks often distract both the leader and the employee from discussing strategy and alignment.

Ensuring that tactical daily efforts align with organizational direction is one of the most important aspects of the leader's role and should be treated as such. Every leader is responsible for conveying the mission of the organization and defining the purpose of the work being completed. Such information must be communicated in an ongoing manner and is critical to individual and organizational success.

Maximizing individual capability is only possible when employees have a clear understanding of the mission to which they are contributing.

Imagine yourself as the captain of a ship that is about to sail around the world. Your crewmembers have been selected, the ship has been stocked and prepared, and the maps for the trip are safely in your possession. The ship begins to sail and crewmembers are busy running about the ship in an effort to ensure a successful launch.

Although the crew when hired was made aware of the overall objective to sail around the world, all discussions since have been centered on the details of preparing the ship for its initial launch.

Once out to sea, the efforts of the crew become more of a routine management of ship operations, each individual focusing solely on his or her specific function. Behaviors slowly turn robotic and the work becomes a daily grind; every day looking the same as the day before. Common goals are not a focus until weather elements or other challenges occur. While the work is accomplished, there is little enthusiasm expressed and the overall mission is overshadowed by day-to-day activities.

Now, imagine what the experience and effort would look like if every crewmember were included in the details of the strategy and mission such as speed and distance needed daily to achieve goals; budgetary requirements for the trip; docking ports along the way and length of stay; anticipated weather challenges. The crew would individually and collectively be far more motivated to achieve the goal. Every day would be an adventure, and just about the time the work became routine, new information would emerge to assist in shifting attention to the overall mission.

Knowing the destination and expectations for the journey promotes teaming and collaboration while at the same time incorporating purpose and meaning into every aspect of the job. Tasks are performed with an increased commitment to outcomes rather than merely to fulfill job expectations in order to collect a paycheck. While pay may be a priority to everyone, it is certainly not the primary factor that drives perceived value.

Leaders in manufacturing organizations were amongst the first in business to recognize the value of meaningful work. Through careful evaluation of the connection between tasks and outcomes, they learned that quality increased with improved understanding of the end result. Understanding this critical factor led to exposing employees to customer satisfaction information and customer input for improved value. This knowledge also led to revamping employee orientation programs to include training on how individual efforts were linked to delivering business results.

Even today in these proactive environments, front line workers are solicited for their input to manufacturing challenges and product improvements. By allowing plant workers to meet with design teams, discussions often lead to increased efficiency in product production and use. Enhancements resulting from these discussions can also lead to financial savings or reduction in defective items and costly recalls. Many companies reward individuals for their ability to find cost savings.

Dedication, commitment, and retention increase with improved understanding of the connection between efforts and outcomes. Every employee, regardless of industry, title, or role, should fully understand and be able to articulate how their specific role fits into the overall scheme of organizational objectives. Understanding the connection between individual contribution and business outcomes increases self-perception of value to the organization, and ultimately improves contribution and commitment.

Although leadership intentions may be favorable in trying to ensure this information is shared with employees, the fact remains that a large percentage of employees cannot clearly communicate how their role impacts the organization. This is particularly true in jobs that are in support of groups that are revenue generators.

It is easy for revenue generating groups to perceive their value to the organization. In these groups, success is often measured by achieving financial goals and value of contributions is highly visible to many people. When the group underperforms and financial goals fall short of expectations, individual contributors can quickly assess what led to success or failure.

When alignment between activities and business objectives is clear, the revenue generators know the targets and can collectively work towards the goal. The organization benefits when a community effort is formed and silos are eliminated.

Employees in support functions must also be able to assimilate how their role contributes to the bottom line. Lack of attention to these less visible roles can mistakenly be perceived by individuals as the organization devaluing the work being performed.

Sharing alignment information is not just about creating and delivering another elaborate slide presentation of projected sales and goals. While it makes sense for the revenue generators to receive forecasts and projections, this same information would offer little relevance to those in support roles.

What needs to be highlighted for the non-revenue generators is the impact of their efforts on the organizational strategy for achieving goals. The focus should be on *how the revenue generators benefit from their assistance and how in turn that assists the organization in meeting its goal.* This information would bring clarity to the relevance of the non-revenue generator's role.

Improved alignment can drive individual growth and development, but it is ultimately the leader's responsibility to ensure this occurs. The question is how to incorporate alignment practices into all efforts within the organization, so it becomes a natural part of daily activities.

THE ALIGNMENT PROCESS

Given time demands on the leader, it can be difficult to add yet one more meeting or to-do item to the calendar. However, taking steps to improve individual understanding of value to the organization would enhance performance and improve effectiveness, making it a worthwhile effort.

The easiest place to begin incorporating alignment is in the interview process. From the very onset of discussions related to any role, leaders should establish the practice of communicating purpose and value. Using the interview as the starting point instills value in the work and sends a clear message to the potential candidate that every job counts in the organization.

Nancy Mercurio

Once the individual is hired, the topic must be revisited in an ongoing manner, both formally and informally. Any opportunity to improve individual perception of contribution and worth will increase commitment to delivering quality work effectively and efficiently.

These ongoing conversations of individual impact to mission and objectives provide greater value than a flashy presentation of information. From weekly update meetings to performance assessment discussions, conversations regarding job value must become standard practice. These conversations help to link each piece of the puzzle to the overall picture, which maintains clarity of purpose and worth.

The example of the ship sailing the world can help clarify this point:

A one-time, formal presentation of the intentions for this mission would have little meaning sixty days after the trip began. However, holding weekly update discussions during the trip to prepare the crew for upcoming challenges and to review navigation plans, would keep them engaged throughout the trip.

Regular staff meetings are a perfect opportunity to share tidbits of information and maintain awareness of organizational mission and strategy. For example, if one of the agenda items for the meeting is to discuss an initiative in progress, invite a volunteer to explain the mission of this initiative to the group. You can also ask for someone to explain the value of the group's role to the mission. In both cases you can provide clarity where needed, but this approach allows you to ensure understanding exists.

Using these small windows of opportunity to keep the mission clear will prevent individuals from being so caught up in the details that they forget the purpose. Additionally, revisiting such relevant information during meetings will maximize use of time, and have a greater impact long-term in ensuring employee engagement in the mission.

EVALUATING EMPLOYEE COMMITMENT

Ensuring alignment also requires maintaining awareness of individual commitment to the process. When personal commitment is reduced, productivity is affected which ultimately impacts the organization and its mission.

Asking if the individual is still committed to the role is ineffective, but you would be surprised to learn how many leaders ask such questions. Clearly the intent behind doing so is to make the individual aware that the leader suspects or has observed a lesser commitment. However, few employees in their right mind would ever reply no when asked, so what is the point?

Assessing commitment is not as easy as evaluating performance, but it can be best accomplished through improved listening. Leaders can check the pulse of the organization by listening carefully to what is going on around them. Casual conversations occur throughout each day and are the simplest means of gaining insight into individual commitment and organizational needs. It takes less energy to listen then it does to implement corrective action plans. Listening requires paying attention long enough to glean key comments and phrases that unveil underlying issues.

Commitment can be evaluated through listening for statements such as: *things were going better before, or I have no idea why we are doing things this way, or no one cares what I think these days.* Leaders often ignore these comments, passing them off as employee complaints or spouting off. However, these statements often indicate potential gaps that exist and signal larger underlying concerns. Taking a few extra moments to further investigate the meaning behind these informal comments can reveal critical information and provide insight into individual and organizational needs.

IMPROVED DECISION MAKING

Aligning efforts with organizational objectives also requires improved decision-making. Although ad hoc decision-making is necessary to keep daily operations in motion, each decision must include consideration of impact to alignment. Whenever possible, leaders should communicate how decisions align with mission and objectives. This is particularly important when decisions involve a change in direction, which employees often misinterpret as a change in the overall mission. Leaders should clarify when course changes impact the strategy of the objectives as employees find it difficult to remain committed to a moving target. Keep the goals clear and be sure employees can articulate them to you in informal opportunities.

When daily efforts align with the organizational mission, employees perceive the purpose in their work. Those who understand how they impact the business objective perform with the highest level of dedication and desire for a quality end result. This can be easily observed with political campaign teams during any type of election. These individuals have a common goal. Regardless of how mundane the task, they perceive the value in their efforts and are reminded constantly of their worth.

Creating an environment that mirrors this practice requires consistent revisiting of purpose, integration of strategy into all activities, and constant reminders of worth to the overall mission. Listening for individual commitment and identifying when clarification is needed are key factors in driving successful alignment of tasks to mission.

While it may take more time and effort initially to incorporate the practice of ensuring all activities are connected to the big picture, the results of adopting this concept have a lasting impact. When the leader exemplifies a consistent practice of intentional and noticeable alignment of all activities, employees will learn that it is also an expectation of them to think in similar terms. Subsequently, they will begin offering feedback on strategic alignment of ideas and activities without being prompted to do so.

When alignment of activities to the mission is naturally integrated into all organizational efforts, employees become more business minded in their approach to tasks. Understanding the organization from a business perspective helps employees more easily adapt to changes in direction.

The value of cultivating a more business minded organization will improve individual growth and development while simultaneously improving overall accomplishments. Being a part of the business mission allows individual contributors to participate in a collective consciousness. It's a win-win for everyone and is indeed preferred over having individuals disconnected from the purpose of their work.

Leaders are responsible for alignment, and alignment leads to responsible behaviors.

CHAPTER 8

Behaving Responsibly in Every Situation

Managing effective and productive organizations requires the ability to behave responsibly. Nothing is more damaging to a leader's reputation than poor decision-making and unprofessional behaviors, and such actions fuel unproductive conversations in the workplace. Stories of leaders and their inappropriate outbursts or public chastising of others spread faster than wildfire in any organization.

Behaving responsibly is a requirement for success in leadership and is not optional. The reputation associated with behaviors (both good and bad), precedes every leader as he or she moves from one role to another within the same organization. Leaders in new roles are either embraced for the anticipated goodness they bring, or are doomed from ever achieving their goals; all because of their reputation.

In all activities, a leader must display responsible behaviors that lend credibility to the leader's skills, demonstrate respect for others, and set an example for others to model. This is indeed an area where *Taking the Elevator Up* is a necessity.

Behaving responsibly can encompass everything from actions in the hallways to the manner in which decisions are made. Every leader is constantly under surveillance by subordinates, peers, and other leaders throughout the organization, and no story is left untold. Employees who witness or overhear the leader in any situation where actions can be perceived as less than professional, are quick to pass their perception along to others.

During the past decade, the public has been inundated with media coverage of leaders who behaved irresponsibly; causing damage to themselves, to others, and to the organizations they served. Story after story has been shared in gruesome detail; each describing yet another leader who made poor choices and crossed the line between ethical and unethical practices. In every scenario, the outcome was a terminally damaged reputation with little hope for reinventing oneself.

To achieve success, leaders must develop a consistent set of practices that serve as the foundation for all of the leader's activities and interactions. Such practices allow for positive and predictable expectations of leader behaviors and eliminate distractions from work.

While it is certainly human to make mistakes, no action is erasable once it has occurred. It is also important to recognize that every incorrect or inappropriate action will require numerous corrective actions; most of which are targeted towards changing the minds of those who witnessed the behaviors.

Behaving responsibly requires the ability to make decisions both impromptu and planned. These decisions must include seeking the highest level of perspective prior to making decisions, and ensuring that all actions are in the best interest of the individual and the organization.

Nancy Mercurio

Decisions must be made with complete objectivity, which is easier said than done. Time constraints and pending deadlines often prevent proper evaluation necessary to make solid and fact-based decisions. As a result, leaders tend to operate more with an act now, think later policy, which historically has produced less than favorable outcomes.

There are numerous occurrences of poorly made decisions that occur daily in organizations around the globe, the majority of which never receive any public attention. While perhaps not media worthy, these inadequate choices receive the attention of many within the organization and can be detrimental to a leader's reputation.

What causes poor decision making?

Over inflated egos and inappropriate use of power are two factors common to leaders who demonstrate poor decision making skills. In some cases, title alone has created unthinking, power-wielding individuals who make spur of the moment decisions without consideration of the consequences or impact.

Employees responsible for the implementation of these decisions, often share the challenges they foresee, but receive little to no attention for their concerns. Over time, these same employees soon learn that sharing an opinion is wasted energy. This realization eventually leads to the practice of implementation without personal investment in the outcome. Sooner or later, even the most talented and loyal contributors become disinterested in helping drive organizational success.

There are many rationalizations for why leaders are unwilling at times to embrace feedback from employees when it comes to decision making. For some it is a matter of not wanting to appear as though the risks being brought to their attention went unnoticed by them. In other cases, it might be a leader's perception that employees cannot possibly comprehend the magnitude of such decisions.

There are also leaders who believe that employees lack the experience needed to understand the business reasons for complex decisions. Yet, on the contrary, it is often the employees who have the greatest insight, particularly when it comes to assessing customer impact.

Another major factor for resistance to employee feedback related to decisions is the timing of the input. Those responsible for implementation may not have been included in the planning stages, thereby making it difficult to incorporate their suggestions once decisions have been set into motion.

Lack of information is also a cause of poor decision-making. Uninformed leaders, who overreact by taking such actions as pulling people from projects or getting involved in a situation prematurely, can cause irreparable damage.

People and organizations are negatively impacted by poor decision-making and the damage is often irreversible. One decision, small or large, can cause a ripple effect, disrupting momentum and effectiveness. In fact, many leaders and organizations spend months recovering from one bad decision.

The most destructive decisions are those that imply or demonstrate sheer disrespect for others or negate past efforts, regardless of outcomes. For example, when announcing a change in direction midstream, some leaders will denounce prior efforts to date in order to justify the new direction. While it may be necessary at times to offer some explanation for a new path, there is no value in communicating that prior efforts have been futile. Few employees are motivated when learning that hard work and long days equate to zero value to the organization.

This is also true in situations where a change in leadership is made on a project already in process and the current leader receives no credit for efforts thus far. No purpose is served in verbally negating work that has been completed, even when a change in direction is in order.

Poor decisions can cause emotional and organizational harm. Therefore, leaders must learn to give careful consideration to the impact of decisions before communicating them.

What leads to good decision making?

Given a leader's reputation is affected by the decisions he or she makes, spending more time on preparations for making decisions is advisable. Such deliberation can be accomplished through conducting a quick assessment of 5 basic questions prior to making any decision:

Assessment #1

Have all the facts been presented, and are those facts clear?

Assessment #2

Are there other individuals who can provide additional insight?

Assessment #3

Who or what will be impacted by the decision and to what extent?

Assessment #4

What risks exist to time constraints or pending deadlines?

Assessment #5

How can the decision be presented in a way that minimizes disruption?

Using these questions will help ensure all facts are gathered, potential obstacles are considered, and impact to the organization is factored into the decision making process. Proper preparation will avoid distracting employees from the work at hand and risking your reputation.

Incorporating these *5 Assessments* into daily decision-making practices will improve business and organizational outcomes. It is a practice worth establishing and an investment that will produce a valuable return.

Another way to improve decision-making is to use a more compassionate approach. On any given day, a leader can peruse the environment and observe employees who are truly invested in their work. Remembering to look for the good in the environment will remind you of the impact your decisions can have when made hastily.

Gaining perspective prior to making decisions is a critical factor to implementation; however, it is only one of many ways in which a leader can learn to behave more responsibly.

Nancy Mercurio

BEHAVING RESPECTFULLY

Many leaders are respected for the title and or position they hold, often times before accomplishments are known. To a new employee, for example, the leader might be viewed as a mentor before mentoring capabilities are displayed. For those without experience or evidence to the contrary, there is an automatic assumption that the leader can provide guidance and insight based on title alone. Over time, the leader's actions either support or negate this belief, which plays a major role in the respect given.

Most interesting is that a leader who demonstrates respect for employees can fail miserably at accomplishments, yet be perceived as successful. Conversely, a leader who demonstrates a lack of respect for employees, but is extremely successful in driving outcomes, is typically not viewed as being successful. It's all a matter of perspective.

The bottom line is that employees will be respectful to those leaders who behave respectfully towards them. Therefore, understanding what factors lead to disrespect is quite valuable in helping shape best practices.

There are several behaviors that can elicit disrespect from employees:

Devaluing Employees, especially in open forums, is a leading catalyst for disrespect. Any occasion where an employee is at risk for ridicule or embarrassment should be avoided. While it is undoubtedly true that there are times when ideas and opinions from an employee seem farfetched, displaying that view can diminish confidence and prevent future input from the individual.

When employees share views that are impractical or even ridiculous sounding, leaders should ask questions that prompt additional development of the concepts. Such responses can include the following:

- *Can you explain further?*

- *Sounds more complicated than we might have time for in this meeting. Can you email the concept to me and/or discuss this with your team first?*

- *Is there a documented plan for what you are suggesting? If so, could I see it?*

- *Not sure we have the time right now to implement something of this nature, but I'd like to see the costs associated with the concept.*

The goal is to help the employee learn from the process of vetting an idea and taking ownership for having raised the issue. This approach also removes the spotlight off you and eliminates the chance of you being seen as uninterested in the idea.

In situations where ideas are shared prematurely without consideration of cost factors or potential for duplication of efforts, this process can be valuable in helping employees reach practical and logical conclusions.

Using this approach eliminates the potential for incomplete ideas to become the responsibility of the leader. It also cultivates an improved process for generating employee suggestions while building solid analytical skills in the organization.

Nancy Mercurio

When the employee has completed the investigation and the idea still warrants additional consideration, the leader must then provide appropriate guidance and encourage follow-up efforts to be managed by the employee when possible. With a careful and compassionate approach, the individual is validated for their efforts and a good idea gains the attention it deserves.

Dismissing Employees, even when unintentional, is another very damaging behavior to a leader's reputation. Employees who feel dismissed are not always willing to try again, which prevents leaders from gaining valuable insights from the talent hired.

Unintentional dismissals occur more than intentional dismissals in the workplace. For example: many leaders are frequently stopped by employees in the hallways in the process of rushing from one meeting to another. Out of respect, the leader stops to acknowledge the individual without having the time to devote to the conversation.

For an employee who feels more confident in a one-on-one setting, this is an easier way to approach the leader on issues. However, without the proper time and attention to devote to the conversation, the employee feels dismissed.

In most cases, the employee will approach the leader and ask a rhetorical question such as, *do you have a minute.* Without waiting for an answer, the employee continues to speak and the one-minute request quickly turns into a fifteen-minute dialogue.

In these situations, it is best to take a different approach. Rather than stopping when unable to give the employee the attention deserved, leaders must learn to be honest and offer an alternative as outlined in the example below:

Employee: *Do you have a minute?*

Leader: *Unfortunately, I don't, and I certainly wouldn't want to be disrespectful by not giving you my full attention. Can you leave me a voicemail about this or drop me an email?*

This approach demonstrates respect for the employee and implies openness to feedback and input.

While many leaders already use a similar honest approach, most will typically offer to take ownership for the follow-up as demonstrated below:

Employee: *Do you have a minute?*

Leader: *Unfortunately, I don't, but I'll give you a call later when I'm back in the office.*

When you take ownership for the follow-up, there is risk in the employee feeling dismissed or devalued. However, if the message to the employee is an invitation to follow-up and the employee chooses not to, then the subject or topic must not have had value to the employee.

In cases where it is suspected that employee shyness or nervousness is the reason for lack of follow-up effort, the leader should initiate conversation to help bridge the gap. Comfort level will improve over time with the leader's assistance.

Gossiping is another behavior to avoid. Too many leaders make the mistake of talking to one individual about another, regardless of who initiates the conversation. When leaders express such opinions, the information travels throughout the organization, perpetuating water cooler conversations and disrupting the workday. Worse yet is that the employee who heard the information from the leader has a false sense of security in perceiving he or she is the leader's confidant. From that moment on, the employee will begin seeking other opportunities to build a closer relationship with the leader, believing all the while that doing so will increase job security. When the relationship becomes strained, the information can be used unwisely and cause problems for the leader.

Even when intentions are favorable, such discussions are often misinterpreted. Much like the telephone game you undoubtedly played at some point in life, every person receiving the information adds their perspective to the existing view. The facts become muddled and someone's reputation is left to interpretation.

What qualifies as gossip?

The answer is quite simple: *anything you are unwilling to repeat to the individual at the center of the conversation should be treated as gossip.*

Clearly, there are times when an individual is the topic of conversation related to a promotion or termination. In these scenarios, the leader holds private conversations with key individuals and the discussions are confidential. Such discussions should not be misconstrued as gossip. When held with the appropriate parties, conversations of this nature are critical to conducting business. The distinguishing factors are intent and purpose, and certainly logic must be applied.

Gossiping is simply lethal to an organization and should be avoided by leaders, and discouraged as a practice amongst employees.

Emotional Reactions, particularly those that are negative, can also damage a leader's reputation. In most situations, emotional reactions are evoked prior to all of the facts being revealed.

The leader's job is to *respond versus react,* and avoid being drawn into the emotional reactions of others. For example, an employee who has just encountered a major obstacle in the process of completing a task is likely to be upset when sharing the news with the leader. If the leader reacts to the news emotionally, the employee's concerns are heightened, and the leader's behavior becomes a distraction from achieving a resolution.

By *responding versus reacting,* the leader creates a safe space for all facts to be uncovered. Maintaining a calm, collective approach, the leader can help the employee remain focused on the issue at hand and together, they can work to resolve the situation.

It is imperative that the leader avoid being the distraction in these scenarios.

Sometimes leaders display emotional reactions when they disagree with organizational decisions. Behaving in this manner encourages disloyalty to the company, tarnishes the leader's image, minimizes contribution, and forces employees to either align with the leader or the organization, rather than both.

As the leader, it is your responsibility to demonstrate an alliance to the organization, even when you disagree with organizational direction. There are ways to align subordinates with organizational decisions and disagree in theory without compromising integrity.

The following sample statements can be used to help staff align with the organization:

While it isn't the obvious direction we had hoped for, we must trust that the organization is doing what is in the best interest of the business and act accordingly.

Although I too was surprised by this decision, I can see how moving in this direction could be beneficial.

We should begin focusing our energy and efforts on helping the organization achieve this goal.

It is certainly okay to admit to employees any uncertainty you may have regarding a decision; however, you should avoid disclosing your full view on the matter. Such discussions can be held privately with your boss.

Lack of Integrity or dishonest practices can create an irreversible disrespect for leaders. The old adage *say what you mean and mean what you say,* is the best practice to adopt. Leaders should avoid saying anything that they cannot fully support or control, as doing so will minimize respect from employees.

Operating with integrity allows employees to trust your word and the fact that they can count on you when needed. For example, if you state or imply that your plans are to grow and develop an employee by year-end, the employee remembers your commitment. In fact, your comments may actually serve as a motivator in helping the employee overcome challenges during the year.

Subsequently, the next time a position is posted in your department, this employee immediately assumes he or she is going to be the candidate chosen. Regardless of the reason, if this employee is not chosen for the promotion, the employee learns to distrust your word.

Acting with integrity requires refraining from making any statements that imply hidden meaning or are not within the leader's authority to take action on. For example, some leaders mistakenly verbalize comments as those listed below:

I'm not at liberty to say at this time, but trust me, there's something pending that will make you very happy.

I've suggested you be considered for an upcoming project, and I'm pretty confident I can influence the decision that you be selected.

There's a chance that you may be traveling to Germany to represent us for a meeting, and you may be able to take your family.

The comments above encourage hopeful expectations and can lead to grave disappointment when they don't come to fruition, even with the best intentions. Although it is certainly understandable that the leader would want to create positive expectations, it is the outcome that matters most to the employee. If the outcome is disappointing, it will far outweigh the joy experienced while holding positive expectations. Although proceeding cautiously may be less encouraging initially, there is less likelihood of long-term damage.

Nancy Mercurio

Leaders are in the spotlight at all times in the workplace and the best behaviors include those that minimize unnecessary attention, keep employees focused, and demonstrate your loyalty to employees and to the organization.

Leaders cannot expect positive behaviors from their employees if they do not model the behaviors themselves. It all boils down to leaders learning to set examples for their employees; acting in ways that they want others to behave.

CHAPTER 9

Employee Behaviors and Perspective

Nothing is more important to successful leadership than learning how to manage employee behaviors. Without employees, there is no purpose for the leader's role! Mission statements, business objectives, and financial goals are all worthless without people to perform the tasks that drive business. The leader's primary responsibility is to nurture and guide employee actions to successful outcomes. Guiding improved behaviors must become a leadership priority.

Employees are the mechanics of the business, thereby making the management of employee behaviors the largest aspect of the leader's role, and often the most time consuming. Oversight for employee actions, and in some cases subsequent damage control, can easily prevent leaders from accomplishing other tasks and cause immense frustration. Discussions, guidance, accolades, troubleshooting, coaching, and performance improvement plans are all measures used to help individuals succeed; all of which require time, attention, and effort.

While there are times when all the proper steps have been taken to ensure success and outcomes are still disappointing, every employee deserves the chance to succeed. Therefore, leaders must make individual growth and development a primary focus.

Nancy Mercurio

Candidates are hired for experience, expertise or perceived potential, all in good faith for a promising future. A financial and personal investment is made in each and every employee to utilize, grow, and develop individual capability. It makes good financial sense to invest the time necessary to develop those hired, and maximize the investment.

Employee growth and development is a benefit to individuals and to the employer, which makes the investment in each individual worthwhile. As skills and aptitude increase, contributions to business needs increase, and this can lead to improved profitability and success.

What's interesting to note is that as time consuming and important as managing employee behaviors is, only a fraction of formal education addresses this topic. A person can graduate with an MBA having taken as few as one or two courses on the subject of human behavior. Beyond requiring leaders to complete classes in Human Relations and Organizational Behavior prior to accepting a managerial position, leaders must rely on trial and error, experience, or training at the company's expense.

Leadership training and executive coaching programs are both popular and viable avenues for leaders to gain new skills and insights into managing employee behaviors. Companies allocate money to training budgets and whether delivered by internal staff or vendors, training programs are beneficial to individuals and to organizations.

For the most part, organizations manage training proactively, particularly when it comes to preparing individuals for upcoming product or program launches. Hiring a coach is often a proactive effort when an individual is transitioning to a new role, or when someone is viewed as having high potential.

However, in many cases, training and coaching efforts are in reaction to something that has gone astray or actions that have raised concerns regarding an individual's skill set. With improved ability to manage employee behaviors, leaders can reduce and even eliminate the aftermath and improve individual and organizational effectiveness.

Nothing is better than a well-oiled machine and the same is true for the workplace. Efficiency and effectiveness are always the goal regardless of industry, which means ensuring that individual contributors give their best and develop a keen sense of business in the process. Helping individuals understand how their actions positively and negatively affect the environment and outcomes is a means of maximizing employee contributions. The leader's efforts are imperative to this process.

Clearly, behaviors that positively affect the environment are the easiest to observe, manage, reward, and reinforce. Employees who are acknowledged for such favorable actions will happily repeat the behaviors and will require few if any reminders to do so. This concept is as simple to understand as Pavlov's Theory; *reinforce the correct behaviors and you bring about more of the same.*

Less favorable behaviors that negatively affect the environment are far more time consuming.

Nancy Mercurio

IDENTIFYING CORRECTIVE ACTIONS

Responding without consideration for what corrective actions would cultivate long-term, behavioral changes, is one of the greatest failures of leadership. Without this critical understanding and ability, leaders find themselves routinely addressing the same problems. It is a practice most commonly known as the insanity principle: *doing the same thing repeatedly, and expecting a different result.* Any leader who wants to be successful must learn this valuable lesson. Addressing the problem correctly the first time will eliminate having to revisit similar issues.

In order to determine the best path for corrective action, the leader must first uncover all facts related to the situation, including behaviors. This information is then used to evaluate the difference between what occurred and what was expected in regards to this deliverable.

It's all about gaining perspective.

Understanding the underlying facts in any challenge is easier when observing the situation first hand; however, the process is more complex when multiple perspectives are involved.

In cases where the situation is observed first hand, the employee and the leader should meet to discuss the circumstances and the actions taken. Through a series of questions and answers, facts can be uncovered. With this information clear, the two can work together to develop an action plan that will resolve the problem. While it is often easier for the leader to direct the corrective action without employee input, it is the collective effort that increases the learning opportunity for the employee.

Questions for uncovering facts and mapping a corrective action plan should include any or all of the following:

> *Can you help me understand what happened? Please be sure to include details even if you think I may already know them.*
>
> *To be sure we are on the same page, can you tell me what you understood as the expectation for this deliverable?*
>
> *At what point in the process did you notice the problem?*
>
> *From your perspective of this situation, what corrective actions are necessary?*

At this point in the conversation, the leader either agrees or disagrees with the corrective actions shared by the employee and should follow one of the paths described below.

If in agreement with the employee's corrective action plan:

> *Sounds like the right direction. What help do you need from me? Please let me know the outcomes of the corrective action ASAP.*

If not in agreement, proceed with questioning:

> *Tell me why you think that this plan will solve the problem.*
>
> *If you do _____ as you are stating, you risk _____. I'd like to suggest that you rethink the situation and offer a solution that mitigates any risks.*
>
> *What problems do you foresee in implementing my recommendations?*

What help do you need from me?

Please let me know the outcomes of the corrective action ASAP.

The goal in this questioning process is to uncover the facts related to the challenge *from the employee's perspective.* There is no doubt that you as the leader could identify and resolve the problem however, there is zero value to the employee in taking that route. Once you understand the challenge from the employee's perspective, you can guide the individual through a logical approach to achieving the best solution. For the leader, the value is in learning about the individual's skill set and ability to comprehend the business needs. For the employee, the value is in having support and proper guidance when needed, while at the same time learning how to better handle such challenges in the future.

The question and answer approach is the preferred method for every situation and will definitely lead to a viable outcome and optimize employee learning. However, there are critical situations that may call for more immediate intervention and direction. In these cases, the leader should take whatever action is necessary to minimize the disruption to business activities.

Avoiding interruptions to business activities takes precedence over addressing individual behaviors or long-term solutions. Once the situation is under control, the leader should hold a conversation with the employee to review the events that led to the problem.

The following question and answer approach is recommended for the post-situation conversation:

Why do you think I stepped in to assist in this situation?

Can you explain why I recommended this corrective action?

From your perspective, what happened to cause this problem?

What other corrective actions do you think might have worked?

What lessons did you learn from this experience that you could use in the future?

This form of debriefing will bring closure to the situation. It provides valuable insights to the leader in identifying skill gaps if any, and helps the individual grow and develop in the process.

Whenever possible, leaders are best suited to guide the employee on how to implement the corrective action as opposed to stepping in and controlling the scene. Doing so will lead to empowerment, and those who are empowered can learn from their mistakes.

UNCOVERING SKILL GAPS

Managing corrective actions requires identifying paths for getting the mission back on course. In the process, deficiencies in employee skill sets are often revealed. These deficiencies must be addressed once business problems are resolved.

In situations where the employee has acted in a manner outside standard operating procedure, reprimand does little to uncover why the employee took this particular course of action. Uncovering this information is as important to the employee as it is to the leader and leads to permanent elimination of unpleasant experiences and useless efforts. Understanding why the action was incorrect is the catalyst for changing the behavior. Therefore, the leader must reveal the source of the problem once business activities have resumed.

The first step is to determine whether actions taken were a result of independent decision-making, or an underlying organizational problem such as poorly written Standard Operating Procedures, improper training, lack of communication, or lack of supervision. Once the source of the problem is identified, a permanent adjustment can be made for long-term, positive impact.

Consider the following example to demonstrate this point:

A group you supervise is responsible for planning an important in-house meeting in which a new marketing strategy for a key product will be introduced.

You return from an unrelated morning meeting and are greeted with the news that marketing materials are already at the printer and everything is on track. Since you have not seen the final copy, you experience a moment of sheer panic. In that brief moment you realize that your direct report is the person responsible for daily oversight of this project and this is a person whose ability you trust. In a calm voice, you ask who signed off for approval on the materials, only to learn that it was someone other than the person you delegated this responsibility to.

Before asking any additional questions, you immediately call the printing department and ask to speak to your contact person there; telling her what happened and asking that the printing be stopped before charges are incurred.

The employee who shared the news is now standing in front of you completely dumbfounded.

What is the source of the problem?

There are numerous possibilities to consider in identifying the source:

- How were expectations related to procedure and sign off for final approval communicated at the onset of the project?

- Who instructed this employee to proceed for sign off and approval?

- Where did the person signing off get their approval?

- Why wasn't the person in charge involved?

- What happened to the person who had the authority to sign off?

At this point, there are two reasons for being upset:

1. This is a major initiative in your area of responsibility and you were not included in the final discussions, nor did you see the final proof. Perhaps you did not communicate your desire to see the final product before printing, or maybe the group failed to include you as requested. Either way, this is likely a source of your frustration.

2. In the process of discussing this with the employee, there was no mention of the person who was designated as the project leader, which could mean that the person failed to perform as expected.

There is also one major factor that may have been overlooked:

Perhaps the project leader was out this day but had already viewed and approved the final copy; had asked that a minor adjustment be made; and then assigned someone else to verify that the change was made before printing. The employee who shared the news with you may be unaware of the project leader's involvement and therefore would not have known to mention it to you. In the meantime, you have stopped the printing process, which could now turn out to be a premature decision.

Clearly, there are several factors to investigate before you can fully understand what went wrong or if in fact anything was wrong. More importantly, your actions in this incident could minimize enthusiasm and initiative from individuals who have been solid contributors to date. No doubt, the employee who shared this information will hesitate before sharing similar news in the future, and if no one acted outside the communicated expectations, repercussions could be monumental.

The key in these situations is to uncover the source of the problem, ask all possible questions, and avoid making assumptions.

In situations where you have conducted a thorough investigation and have discovered that behaviors have fallen short of expectations, there are several steps you can take:

STEP 1
Implement immediate corrective actions to maintain business continuity, engaging the employee's assistance whenever possible.

STEP 2
Identify the gap between expectation and performance, uncovering the source of the problem.

STEP 3
Implement a permanent corrective action.

STEP 4
Communicate the incorrect and correct action to everyone involved.

In what other ways do leader behaviors impact employee behaviors?

In any organization, the leader's actions play a huge role in setting the stage for work to be accomplished. In a matter of seconds, a comment or action can turn a good day into an unproductive one. Therefore, it is the leader's responsibility to maintain an atmosphere conducive to productivity by avoiding actions that are disruptive as outlined below:

Infraction #1—*Inconsistent Practices*

The most commonly complained about leadership behavior and greatest frustration to employees is inconsistent practices. Employees find it impossible to accomplish tasks when the leader is constantly changing the game plan or approach to managing tasks and situations. Inconsistency can cause immense disrespect for even the finest of leaders.

Leaders must take every measure possible to operate with consistency in all efforts and eliminate any chance for interpretation of inconsistent practices.

Infraction #2—*Emotional Outbursts*

> When leaders are faced with situations where employee behaviors have fallen short of expectations, emotional responses do little to correct the course of action. In fact, emotional reactions can actually cause more delay in achieving resolution because the employee becomes distracted by the leader's reaction. Such behaviors are ineffective and unproductive.

Leaders can be passionately concerned and manage a situation to a successful conclusion without an overt display of negative emotions.

Infraction #3—*Processing Thoughts Out Loud*

> Many employees listen to EVERY word the leader says and subsequently will become confused when too much information is shared, never asking for clarity. As a result, actions are taken based upon employee interpretation of the most relevant point communicated. Processing out loud can also leave the leader accountable when incorrect actions are taken.

> Leaders should take the time necessary to process thoughts alone before providing guidance unless the effort is intentionally collaborative.

Infraction #4—*Clichés*

Some leaders use clichés to express their desires for action without defining what is actually intended. There are several such phrases commonly used by leaders, all of which can offer little value to employees:

> *Pull it together*
> *Step it up*
> *Make it happen*
> *Get it done*

While each of these sample phrases may imply a leader's concern for pending deadlines or unfinished work, interpretation of relative importance is left to employee perception. Without clarity surrounding expectations, deadlines are missed and the behaviors are repeated by employees.

Leaders should adopt the practice of communicating exactly what is needed and expected, including concerns regarding upcoming deadlines. Say what you mean and mean what you say is the rule to abide by.

What feedback is most useful to improving employee behaviors?

Behaviors are best modified when the individual receives useful guidance intended to help direct improved actions. Such feedback is targeted towards driving permanent versus temporary changes in behavior.

Nancy Mercurio

Constructive feedback conveys a view in a manner intended to help an individual without belittling or embarrassing, and includes basic components that accomplish the following:

1. Clearly identifies the incorrect action.
2. Explains why the action is incorrect.
3. Guides or directs the correct action (depends on employee knowledge).
4. Ensures understanding.

Example of constructive feedback:

While calling the customer to correct the situation is the right action, the call was placed before you had properly analyzed the facts and developed some potential solutions to share with the customer. By calling prematurely, you had to place the customer on hold and get the answers you needed, which made you appear less competent to the customer. Next time, use the facts you have to investigate possible solutions so you can be prepared to offer them without interruption to the call. Any questions?

With this approach, the leader helps the individual understand what actions can be improved upon and how to approach a similar situation in the future.

To drive effective changes in employee behaviors, leaders must become fully aware of the impact their actions have on others. Employees watch, listen and act according to what they believe is the leader's desire for the organization and for them as individuals. When actions fall short of expectations, there is a reason for the behavior and the gap between what was expected and what was delivered must be addressed.

Behaviors only change when the gap is addressed.

As the leader, you have the power and influence to groom employee behaviors in a way that builds effective teams and organizations. Use that power wisely to guide improved actions, and employee growth and development will flourish.

CHAPTER 10

The Corporate Gandhi

The topic of leadership is an endless sea of opportunity for journalism, particularly as related to the impact leaders have on individuals and organizations. Whether negative or positive, the actions of leaders fuel discussions all around the globe in every language and across cultures. Nothing has greater impact on the success of a business than leadership, so it's worth talking about.

With every position of authority, there are unspoken responsibilities the leader must willingly embrace. Such responsibilities include displaying the professional and humanistic qualities expected from others. Through demonstrating these qualities and behaving in stable and consistent ways, the leader can lead the flock to successful outcomes. Expectations for these demonstrated qualities increase with enhanced responsibility, and at no time is displaying poor judgment an acceptable quality.

For decades, all indicators point towards the fact that leaders are actually a key factor in influencing employee engagement. Translated, it means that *positive leader behaviors drive increased employee engagement.* Given the enormous amount of attention this topic has received over the years, why aren't all leaders acting in ways that drive successful organizations?

The goal for every leader should be to drive success through improved behaviors whether their own or the employee's. Doing so begins with acting in a level-headed manner; addressing all situations with a calm and methodical approach; using facts and objectives as the foundation for developing solutions.

This peaceful demeanor, coupled with the ability to act with integrity, and clarity surrounding roles and targeted goals, is what defines *The Corporate Gandhi*. It is a style proven to be successful by the historically infamous leader Mahatma Gandhi.

Gandhi was a man of wisdom, honor, truth, and peaceful solutions, and he was able to get people to follow him and support his mission through his actions and his words. There was always a higher purpose for everything he did, and people believed in him because of his expressed conviction when speaking. Gandhi's presence exuded the values he asked others to embrace. His practices were unwavering from the goals he committed to, and his actions were consistent regardless of where he traveled. He was a man who captured people's attention and enlisted their support through the example he set.

While there are many leaders who have had shining moments that included acting levelheaded and demonstrating peaceful and solution-oriented behaviors, only a small percentage maintain consistency in displaying such practices. In fact, many leaders allow each situation to dictate their behaviors rather than establishing a consistent set of behaviors to handle all situations. Subsequently, as the seriousness of the situation increases, more disruptive leader behaviors are revealed. Given human tendency to recall the negative, it is these disruptive behaviors that leave leaders with tarnished reputations.

Nancy Mercurio

The Corporate Gandhi is not a leader who wears jeans and a tie-dyed shirt and sings Kumbaya with the team every morning, but rather the individual who is the greatest provider of perspective. Amidst the hectic pace, constant questions and trouble-shooting that occurs in the workplace, this individual is able to *stop, look, listen, and offer sage advice.* Through these actions, the leader is able to minimize disruptions while keeping individuals and activities in forward motion.

For leaders who work in organizations that reward the most aggressive individuals, this peaceful approach may sound like a Catch22 situation. However, it is important to note that such aggressive leaders, who move heaven and earth to accomplish monumental feats, are often those who leave a wake of unresolved issues in the process. For those leaders who actually are successful in achieving lofty objectives while creating chaos, taking a calm and calculated approach to situations might seem like an unnecessary time consumption that stands in the way of business success.

Determining factors for adopting a Gandhi approach is best revealed through the process of conducting an honest self-evaluation of how leadership practices are impacting the organization. It all boils down to whether or not current actions are working for or against you as a leader and the impact those actions are having on those around you.

The proverbial leader is one who can be the daily quarterback in carrying the team, and possess the capability to play tennis at hockey speed when it comes to managing challenges. It is a balancing act predominantly dependent upon one's ability to understand the damage that can occur without such practices in place.

The Corporate Gandhi embraces qualities that may resemble those of a superhero; demonstrates immense courage, acts with integrity, shows respect for mankind, is humble and yet able to leap tall buildings in a single bound (helpful, but not required!). These qualities, when displayed consistently, exude a level of confidence which in turn reassures employees that all is well in spite of appearances; *that objects in the mirror really do appear larger than reality!*

Although the concept of the superhero is used as a reference point to demonstrate the importance of the leader's role, the message is not intended to encourage leaders to save the world. Anyone with leadership qualities knows only too well the damage that can be done when managing as the superhero; *trying to be everything to everyone.* The intended message is for leaders to capture the essence of the superhero in order to instill confidence in employees.

Such traits, when exhibited consistently by many leaders in the same environment, will help define the organization and even increase customer confidence. When customers are confident in the company's ability, they become increasingly more loyal during challenging times.

How can managing with a peaceful presence improve day to day activities and the work flow?

The most important factor is the obvious one: *low stress.* A levelheaded, peaceful, and factual approach to every situation is going to reduce stress for the leader and for the employees. When stress in the organization is minimized, individuals are more productive, and *productivity drives profits.*

There is enough stress associated with meeting targeted sales and operational goals, staying competitive in the marketplace, and driving profitable businesses. Managing with a peaceful presence helps those you lead think more clearly and be more responsive versus reactive to internal and external customer needs. When deadlines are fast approaching or last minute changes are required, a state of calmness combined with the ability to provide perspective will help individuals be creative in driving solutions.

This mode of operations also elicits greater receptivity to new ideas shared by the leader. When suggestions are shared without elevated vocal tones or tense facial expressions, employees are able to listen with an open mind. Consequently, less time is spent helping people understand, and focus remains on addressing the tasks at hand. A levelheaded, methodical, and peaceful approach to situations is the quickest means of achieving a goal, because it is the least distracting. When individuals are distracted by the leader's behaviors, little can be accomplished.

A peaceful presence also keeps the organization moving in a forward direction because issues are addressed without creating additional challenges. While some level of conflict is healthy and can lead to solid business solutions, the majority of challenges are distractions for getting the work accomplished.

What other qualities does The Corporate Gandhi exhibit?

Beyond having a peaceful presence, the most important quality is the ability to *bring clarity to every situation*; acting as the guiding light, paving the pathway for solutions to occur. Providing perspective can often open the door to improved thoughts and actions, and ultimately improve the way business objectives are accomplished.

The leader who brings perspective to every situation can assist in the following ways:

Identifying Challenges
With improved perspective, problems can be isolated, allowing troubleshooting to occur while bringing clarity to the fact-finding mission.

Encouraging Solutions
By providing a clear perspective of the goals and overall mission, employees can focus their attention and efforts on reaching viable solutions.

Teaching Lessons
A peaceful approach combined with the ability to provide clarity, minimizes defensive responses from others, and allows learning to occur.

Leaders capable of providing perspective in all efforts are able to serve as a voice of reason to those who are too immersed in the challenges at hand. This ability to be unshaken by sudden change or news of pending change, models behaviors that help employees learn to respond to change in the same manner. If the leader is observed as being nonchalant when transformation begins, the response from staff will be quite similar.

While most organizations are constantly evolving in order to optimize growth and market positioning, it can be difficult for employees to endure constant change. When changes are initiated at every intersection, or are a result of the organization over-compensating in response to challenges, employee perspective is even less favorable. During these times, the person who can provide the greatest clarity and act as the voice of reason, is the best candidate for helping get individuals and business objectives back on track.

Knowing the impact one person can have on the emotional well-being of the organization should serve as a catalyst for doing what is in everyone's best interest. Leaders must learn to provide clarity and help others learn to do the same.

How does the leader benefit from behaving as The Corporate Gandhi?

The greatest personal benefit of behaving in this manner is the ability to impact others in such a positive and healthy way. Contributing to the physical and mental well-being of individuals and the organization overall is personally rewarding. There are tremendous health benefits that result from creating an environment that operates peacefully. With less stress at work and healthier surroundings, you as the leader are more useful throughout the day as a contributor and may even find yourself singing to the radio on the drive home!

Leading with a calm and peaceful manner will absolutely improve work life balance in the organization. Both leaders and employees will be better prepared to manage challenges at home as a result of experiencing more peaceful surroundings at work.

Acting as a voice of reason and providing perspective and clarity, will elicit greater respect for your input. Sharing your wise and proven ways in a clear, pointed, yet humble manner is preferred. The most aggressive, assertive or capable leaders often experience less receptivity to new ideas they share, when their presence overpowers the words they impart. Taking an approach that is motivating yet humble will require less energy and effort in gaining support and driving implementation.

Keeping the facts clear and at the forefront of all efforts will help pave the way to solutions. People are easily distracted by the details of what surrounds any issue. In many scenarios, actions taken as a result of a situation are more in response to symptoms, rather than in response to the core problem. With the facts clear, the best solutions can emerge and the long-term impact will be beneficial.

How do you know if you already possess attributes of The Corporate Gandhi?

There are a series of questions to ask yourself in factoring what level of peaceful, levelheaded practices you bring to your current surroundings:

- What is your stress level at the end of the day?

- What is the stress level of your employees at the end of the day?

- What level of camaraderie occurs without your encouragement?

- How often are you acting as a mediator?

- How often are solutions presented to you versus sought by you?

- How effective are group meetings in producing results collectively?

These are not trick questions, nor is there a secret formula for uncovering the answers; however, the pattern of thought should be obvious:

If the environment is not as peaceful and productive as it could be, then surely displaying a more levelheaded perspective will improve the atmosphere.

No leader can be held fully accountable for the difference between an employee who joyfully contributes each day, and the one who completes just enough work to collect a paycheck. While the leader is likely an influencing factor, it is important to recognize that every situation is a two-way street. Employees must take some ownership for their willingness to contribute their best, and for the attitude behind their efforts.

However, if more than 50% of the staff in an organization is underperforming, it is fair to assume leadership is likely a contributing factor to the problem. Negative influence can be as subtle as the perception that leadership lacks interest in the employees, or as blatant as a few leaders behaving in less than favorable ways. Regardless, leader behaviors, or a lack thereof, can play a role and must be adjusted in order to drive improved productivity.

The key is to assess the overall climate and analyze the impact of your actions on the environment. With that understanding, you can course correct accordingly while slowly and consistently bringing a peaceful perspective and demeanor to the workplace. Consistency is important because sudden and inconsistent changes will only lead to more problems.

Acquiring the savvy of *The Corporate Gandhi* is not intended to create an untouchable image. The goal is for leaders to master the art of behaving in ways that keep everyone engaged, and all objectives clear and on track for timely completion. This concept is also not intended to create leaders who walk around with their heads in the clouds, a smile on their face and a fire extinguisher in their hand. Nor is the image being recommended one of merely existing for the purpose of keeping the peace or creating a harmonious environment.

What is desired and encouraged is adopting a leadership mindset and establishing practices that are based on one simple principle:

Distractions and disruptions prevent productivity. Minimize the distractions and disruptions and you maximize productivity.

The Corporate Gandhi, therefore, is the leader who at all times can identify what interruptions exist to the workflow, and develop ways to move employees past those disruptions.

Your ability to create an environment where the truth can easily be shared is also a significant and valuable attribute. No one feared speaking to Gandhi. If employees feel free to speak openly and truthfully about the situations they encounter, the path to uncovering solutions is much quicker. On the contrary, if employees feel they must hide the truth from their leader, problems linger, and business outcomes are delayed. The sooner the truth can be shared, the easier it is to maintain business momentum. The leader who understands this relevant factor will experience greater success in producing positive business outcomes.

123

It is imperative to keep a relatively close eye on the environment you manage and participate proactively whenever possible. This does not imply the need to have a hand in all activities, but rather the responsibility for maintaining a 25,000-foot perspective at all times. It is not necessary to operate at a tactical level where you are privy to every detail. However, operating at a strategic level allows you to retain current knowledge for your areas of responsibility while helping to drive organizational success.

Some leaders are notorious for becoming highly involved in certain aspects of the work within their areas of responsibility, while at other times demonstrating a complete lack of interest for similar aspects. This practice sends a message to employees that the leader lacks genuine interest in the work and can place a wedge between employees and the leader; even when untrue.

Displaying a consistent level of interest in all facets of the work you supervise is recommended, and doing so will prevent highs and lows in productivity. It is similar to having a steady metabolic rate where periods of high and low energy are eliminated through eating at consistent intervals throughout the day. With improved consistency,the leadership process is less exhausting and demanding, and work flow remains at a steady pace.

Many leaders question whether these desired behaviors are learned or the result of stellar DNA. Quite frankly, who cares? The bottom line is that without a peaceful presence and the ability to offer perspective throughout the day, work is nothing short of a daily grind.

Improving your practices will change the way your team contributes, and ultimately improve productivity and profitability; especially once the concept and results begin to peak interest. As your peers observe the positive effects of your efforts, they too will want to model the same behaviors. In record speed, *The Corporate Gandhi* approach will permeate the organization.

Begin the journey now towards making personal, behavioral, and organizational improvements, and you will quickly *Elevate Yourself For Success!*

CPSIA information can be obtained at www.ICGtesting.com
Printed in the USA
LVOW120732070912

297640LV00001B/332/P